DATE DUE

Of Time and an Island

John Keats

CHARTERHOUSE
NEW YORK

OF TIME AND AN ISLAND

Foreword

Our house is built on a rock in a river. The rock is one of the oldest known to exist, and you can see on the boulders that emerge from the grasses and the berry bushes and lie about the roots of the trees how the stone swirled and bubbled as it cooled for uncounted years in a time before life began. The river was formed in a subsequent cataclysm witnessed by no living thing. A crack, fifteen hundred miles long, opened in the earth's crust, and water rushed into it.

You can see, on what was once molten stone, the marks the last glacier made. The ice moved over our island just a moment ago in geological time, and nothing else has marked or substantially changed the shape of the island since, for the river carries no cutting instruments and so there is no erosion. The island will remain almost exactly as you see it now, until the next glacier comes.

Our house, however, is less substantial. It could blow away in a wind and very nearly did one summer night while we huddled around the fireplace, thinking that the safest place to be, feeling the house shaking in the hurricane and hearing through the wind the dreadful crack and whump of an enormous white pine breaking and falling on rock. At any instant in a thunderstorm, lightning could set our house on fire, and if we survived the brilliant terror of the bolt itself, we could do little else thereafter but run out into the rain and watch the house burn down. During any winter, ice could lift our house, and, if the ice began to move in wind and current, the house, once lifted, would be carried slowly and inexorably from the rock and down the river to be torn apart when the floe began to heave and break. Then there would be no more trace of our having lived on our island than there are traces of the long-extinct animals that once moved over the ancient stone before the years of man.

Each year for twenty years I have lived with my wife and children alone on our island, and we have drawn a strange comfort from a timeless world compounded of earth, air, fire, and water. Living close prisoner to the four classic elements, or living the close prisoner of a religion, helps anyone to be free to be himself. Twenty years ago we did not know this, but from the first moment we stood on the ancient stone beneath the wind-shaped pines and looked down miles of glinting ice and water, we were sure that we were in the presence of a mystery.

PART ONE

Winter

I

We had never seen the St. Lawrence River in winter until the day we went to look at the island. It was one of those absolutely clear, bright days when you can see for miles, and the details of distant islands and shorelines appeared as small and perfect as an image in the wrong end of a telescope. We stood on the porch of a small wooden cottage built atop a great gray boulder and admired the view. The farthest islands seemed to float on the horizon between sky and water. It was very cold. The bright sun had no weight in it.

"It was right here on this porch that we closed the deal," Bob said. "The fellow wanted fifty-five hundred for the island and the boats. I wrote him out a check for four thousand and handed it to him, and he looked at it for a while. Then he put out his hand and said, 'Mister, you've just bought a very nice island.' "

We could see a great white pine down but still green. Huge stones were tangled in its roots. Everywhere there was a litter of dead branches. It was a rough island that no one had ever tried to garden, two acres of whatever God allowed to grow there, any way it wished. The path we had taken had been worn rather than made through a jungle of raspberry canes and sumacs. Along the path were lampposts made of lead pipe, connected by a cable laid on the surface of the ground. Naked bulbs, some of them broken, were screwed into sockets at the ends of the pipes, and this festive array, rising out of the winter-dead vegetation, led from a broken-roofed boathouse to the cottage atop the boulder.

"What brought the price down?" I wondered.

"I suppose," Bob said, "it was because the island had been up for sale and nobody had turned up to buy it, and he was ill and old and needed the money.

"But the funny thing was," Bob said, brightening at the memory, "that when we got back to Rockport, there was a man waiting on the dock by Collins' store. He had come all the way from New York to buy the island, and he was ready to meet the price. But the owner had my check and we had shaken hands and had a deal."

"What did you do?" my wife asked her brother.

"There wasn't anything they could do about it," Bob explained. "I felt sorry for the owner, but we had a deal. We went right to Escott and transferred the title."

So now Bob had a very nice two-acre island that he

did not want. What he wanted were the three boats that had been sold with the island as part of the deal: the twenty-one-foot cabin launch we had come out in, a twenty-eight-foot Gar Wood speedboat, a sixteen-foot sloop. He wanted us to have the island.

He found the right key and unlocked the padlock on the cottage door. A single square room, its walls and ceiling paneled in pine, contained two brass bedsteads with flat metal springs and thin horsehair mattresses. The seven windows each framed a different picture of trees, blue water, and islands with ice glittering along their shores. Bob said the telephone on the wall was connected only to the boathouse. The parents had used this as a sleeping cottage to escape the noise of the eight children who lived in the boathouse, and the telephone called them to breakfast.

"Let's see the boathouse," Margaret said.

"I have something I want to show you first," Bob said.

"What is that?"

"Just wait till you see," he promised.

With an air of great mystery, Bob led us back not along the path but up through a forest of leafless sumacs, over great gray glaciated stones that formed the exposed spine of the island, and down these to an outbuilding the size of one of those nineteenth-century dollhouses large enough for little girls in crinoline to play in.

His secret was two old Chevrolet automobile engines mounted on concrete blocks inside the dollhouse. They generated electricity. One wall of the house was a puzzle of dials that registered ohms, kilowatts, amperes, and, for all I knew, ergs. The other walls were lined with shelves filled with bits of wire, tubing, rags, paint cans, hopelessly congealed paintbrushes, bottles of screws and nails, trays of old gaskets, rusting tools, and anonymous bits of metal. The cement floor was stained with oil, and it all smelled like a garage.

"All you have to do is throw a switch," Bob revealed.

He pulled on a D-ring, and one of the engines hiccoughed tentatively before expiring in a series of gasps.

"It's cold," Bob explained, "but I know they work. Will and I had them working when I bought the place. In the house, all you have to do is turn a light switch, and the engine starts automatically. The whole place is wired. You saw the line that runs to the cottage at the head of the island."

"Let's see the boathouse," Margaret suggested. She wanted to see the living quarters.

"You'll have to wait," her brother teased.

Close to the engine house was a two-story building, double-walled and insulated, that had once been an icehouse. Wooden slat bunks with drawers for clothing beneath had been built against the pine board walls. Laid over the bed slats were pallets that smelled of wet straw.

"The eight boys and their friends slept out here," Bob disclosed.

"They must have been tired," I said.

"Anyone with eight children would be," Margaret agreed.

"I meant the boys. You have to be tired to sleep on those boards."

"Let me show you the boathouse," Bob said.

6

We walked through and over blowdown and dead leaves along a catwalk of decking. There were rotten boards on the catwalk, and midway along it stood an outhouse with a half-moon slit in its door. A filthy wash-basin, a dirty flush toilet, and a wasps' nest were the principal features of this structure, from which a cast-iron soil pipe ran over the rocks and down to the river. Because the river was low in winter, the pipe hung out over the shore ice.

"I bet you never saw an outhouse with running water before," Bob said.

The boathouse was built in the river on a foundation of stone-filled, plank-floored cribs made of oak timbers. It was a two-story structure typical of the region, fifty feet long and thirty wide. The sills, which at the land end rested on the island rock, ran out over these cribs. The ice would lift such boathouses, and each spring when the ice went out the houses would (hopefully) settle back into place. We saw again the break in the roofline. A porch had been added to the downriver end of the upper story, and the weight of it was breaking the roof.

We entered the living quarters from the catwalk, through the back kitchen door. The kitchen was small and dark, a little room whose pine-paneled walls had been stained dark brown. It smelled of coal oil. All the appliances operated on kerosene: the huge zinc-lined refrigerator chest, the kitchen range of cast iron, and the hot-water heater. The walls above the hot-water heater were scorched black—by fire, not by soot.

Next to the kitchen was a dining porch, evidently put up as an afterthought along the east wall of the boathouse, since the wall was built of outside clapboards. Here through the unshuttered swing-up windows spilled a wonderful bright winter light, and for the first time something began to make sense to me. Just a little elevation made all the difference. When you are on water you are at the bottom of a world that rises all around you. But when you stand above water, even the mere fifteen feet or so that the dining porch was above the river, the world is at your bidding. The north end of the porch projected over water and felt like the bridge of a ship. Double glass doors led from this end of the porch onto the one whose weight was breaking the roof. We pressed our faces against the glass to peer into the dark cavern that had been shuttered against the winter storms.

There was a door to the living room. Bob flicked a light switch, and nothing happened. Prepared, however, for disappointment, he produced a flashlight. The room was huge, dank, and musty. It was bitter cold in the shuttered dark, much colder than in the thin sunlight. The room was immense, running the full width of the boathouse. A large fireplace with some fire bricks missing dominated the east wall. The people who lived here must have adored brown—or perhaps they raised mushrooms—for the walls and ceiling were all stained a dark brown, and there were sepia prints of the Black Forest and of "The Young Violinist" enclosed in even darker brown frames. The walls and ceiling were made of beaverboard, and the ceiling sections billowed from the weight of pools of water that had formed from the leaks in the roof.

The furniture, too, was dark brown. The bookcase,

8

the three flip-top tables with veneer peeling, the sofa and the two chairs with wet, mold-smelling cushions, all these were dark brown and so was the bare floor. But the principal piece of furniture glistened in the flashlight. A table ten feet long and a yard wide rested on a trestle. The grain of the two-inch oak planks was so carefully matched and the planks themselves were so cunningly fitted together that the table seemed a single slab of oak. This table obviously belonged on the dining porch instead of the little pine horror we had seen there. While I ran my fingers along the table top, silently congratulating the prior owners for having had sufficient absence of mind not to stain this but to have used a clear varnish instead, there was a whirr, a clank, and a scratching noise that gave way to a reedy orchestral introduction to Caruso's incredible voice.

We stood silent in the flashlit gloom of an empty dark brown room and, listening to *"La Bella Figlia dell' Amore,"* saw the bright sea and the terraced vineyards. Even on the thick, one-sided disks and for all the surface scratch, the blunt steel needle, and the internal noises of the machine, Caruso managed to fill the room with warmth and color. This old wind-up Victor Talking Machine, with its colophon of the terrier listening to His Master's Voice, and with its cabinet filled with albums of Caruso and Galli-Curci and others from George White's *Scandals,* was another of Bob Bodine's little surprises and by long odds the best of them.

The rest of the second story of the boathouse consisted of four dark-brown bedrooms and, thank God, an indoor bathroom. All of them gave off a narrow dark-brown hall. We shone the light down this mole tunnel and into the shuttered rooms and found the three iron bedsteads and the one brass one—all with horsehair mattresses and flat iron springs—crucifixes above the beds, and the cheap bureaus bought from Montgomery Ward catalogues of the 1920s. The house was completely furnished, down to salt and pepper still in the shakers. There were several incomplete sets of crockery and a flyswatter. As Bob explained, all we had to do to move right in was open the shutters.

A thin wind was gathering strength when we emerged into the winter light. We went out the kitchen door because a tremendous white pine was lying across the stairs that led to what was properly the boathouse front door, at the end of that dark hall. Margaret and I were young and reasonably athletic, but, bulky in our parkas, we climbed awkwardly through the tangle onto the broken side dock to which Bob's cabin launch was moored. The summer past the water had been abnormally high. Someone had put stones on top of the dock to hold it there, but the water had been strong enough to lift both planks and stones. Waves would have built up during summer winds. Standing with miles of open water all about, this was an island that would receive any wind that blew, and every wave. The Thousand Island region is a place of storms—of equinoctial storms that come sliding over the surface of the earth when the world tilts, of summer thunderstorms and winter gales. Repairing storm damage would be the principal recreation of an insular existence. We could see clearly enough what the last storm had done.

We motored slowly away, looking at the island really for the first time. We had fished around it in summer, but then we had been intent only on the colors of the water that indicate the depths, on the distance from weedbeds to shoreline, on dipping the rod tips beneath driftweed. Nor had we paid close attention to the island as we neared it on this winter day. But now that we had walked upon it and had seen its buildings, we looked at it with different eyes. This great bulk of lichened gneiss rose steeply from the cold water; ice glinted on the stone just above the water line. Now we could see it wholly—the stone; the gray skeletons of the sumacs; the white and black of naked birches; the stark forms of oaks and maples; the dead summer grasses a yellow brown; the enormous white pines whose branches, warped by the south wind, were a Japanese etching against the cold and empty sky.

"There's a lot to be done," my wife said.

Margaret was looking at bald patches of roof where shingles had been. Her brother agreed that there was a certain amount of tidying up to do.

We moved slowly, the engine throttled well back, for the gathering wind was cold enough without our adding to it, and there was floating ice in the channel. We stayed carefully well off the downwind side of one large floe. There were two big ravens on it, eating a dead perch. They paid no attention to us. The village of Rockport, more than a mile away, looked as though it belonged beneath a Christmas tree. The sun was bright upon the newly cleaned white statue of the Virgin standing on a rock before the white clapboard church.

We skirted the ice that lay off the foot of Club Island, then coasted beneath cliffs where small cedars sought to root themselves in the frost cracks, to find another boat moving up against the current on the otherwise deserted river.

We came alongside this leaky, creaking thing of unpainted gray weathered boards. In it was a farmer we knew from summers past.

"Any luck?" I asked.

"Oh, I got a few," he said.

We admired the five fat dark-brown bodies stiffening on the wet boards beside his boots.

"What will they bring this year, David?"

He moved uncomfortably as he thought.

"Dollar. Dollar to a dollar twenty-five."

"They look fine."

"They're good enough, but I don't know. They say the price fell out of them. Are you up long?"

"Just for the weekend. We went to look at the island."

"Them two came from there," David said, nudging two of the bodies. "I was there this morning. It's one of my islands."

"Well," I said, "good luck."

"Ehup," he agreed.

We talked no longer. The boats were drifting in the current, and he would have to make up the distance. We had been holding the gunwales of the boats but now pushed them apart, and David Farrer smiled his big, slow smile at us, leaning into his oars. He was a large, broad-faced man, slow in all his movements, who wore only rubber boots, thin work trousers, and a threadbare Mackinaw over a wool-and-cotton shirt. His thick hands were mottled pink and purple, and thin ice formed sparkling on his oar blades as he swept them out of the dark water and up against the wind. David did not have weekends. He had another ten miles to go on his trapline, and rowing would keep him as warm as he would be that day.

David had called it one of his islands, though in fact he owned only a few cows and a small farm whose fields were chiefly glaciated boulders and juniper bushes. His islands were territories assigned to him by the game authorities when he bought his trapping license. They were his to trap if the legal owners had no objection. None of the owners objected for the very good reason they were never asked, and if they had been asked, most of them would have been surprised to learn that people trapped muskrats. Then they might have said no. The owners were Summer People who played golf in the sunshine, ran around the river in speedboats, lived in cities most of the year, and drank more money in a month than many people earn in twelve. David Farrer and his fellow trappers spent their winter days rowing around the river in punts, or walking across it when the ice held, handling their rusting icy chains, prizing the iron jaws apart with stiff fingers, resetting their traps, sometimes finding five rats in one day, only to discover the price had fallen out of the rats. Still, when you have a wife and three children to feed and a farm full of stones, trapping helps. In that case, the islands might belong more to you than to anybody else. Bob wanted to sell us the island he had bought, but as I watched David row slowly against the current in the icewater, it occurred to me to wonder if he could.

It was a thought that tugged at the corners of my mind that evening. With Bob and his wife, Kate, we had a drink before the fire while Bob grilled a steak over embers. Later, we played bridge. We did not discuss the island because we all understood the terms of Bob's proposal. He knew we loved the river. His sister had spent her childhood summers here. Margaret and I had married during the war, and every summer since we had come to spend my two-week vacation on the river, fishing and swimming and drawing breath in the cool Canadian silences until we had to return to the city. We stayed in this summer house, which had belonged to her grandfather and which now belonged to Bob. If we had a place of our own on the river, then we would no longer have to share the mainland house with Bob and his family, which would be mutually convenient. Indeed, this was a reason why Bob had telephoned to us in Maryland, asking if we wanted to come look at an island he had just bought. If we did not want it, he would gladly sell it to someone else for much more money than he had paid for it. The price of island properties was actually rising, not falling; he had been lucky and could afford to wait. He had potential customers in mind. But since we were family and because Bob liked to keep things in the family, he was willing to sell us the island for what he had paid for it—minus the boats. Bob was a Philadelphia stockbroker. In the game businessmen play, money and the things money can buy are the counters they use to keep

score. When he sold the island, either to us or to someone else, Bob would be ahead by three free boats.

In the game I play you keep score differently. I was
not a businessman. I was a Washington newspaper re-
porter. I had nothing in a bank. Margaret and I lived
from Monday to Monday on my weekly wages. The
money Bob wanted us to pay for his island was almost
exactly the sum I earned in a year.

The island was, moreover, ruinous. Even if Margaret and I had the time to do most of the labor ourselves,
the cost of making necessary repairs to the houses and
dock might very well equal the purchase price.

We did not drive up from Maryland with the inten-
tion of buying an island. We had come to spend a winter
weekend on the river to look at the island Bob had
bought; we were curious to see it and glad to enjoy a
break in our winter routine. After all, we could hardly
spend money we did not have to buy something we could
not afford to maintain and, it seemed, we would be
unable to use more often than a fortnight each year. The
economics of the matter simply forbade rational discussion.

Yet there is something about an island that stands
outside rational discourse, just as, in a physical sense, an
island stands apart from all the rest of the world.

Moreover, meeting David Farrer with his muskrats
suggested something else: You could not buy or sell
winter light, freezing water, or cold, clean air. The Indians were certainly right about that. They had no idea that
land could be sold any more than air or water could.

They thought the earth was eternal, designed to be used by everyone while he lived and then by others after him, generation upon generation through time without end. By everyone they meant to include their brothers the animals, the birds, the fishes, the trees, and all living things. The earth and life were to be shared, not sold. It was a point of view that made a great deal of trouble for the Indians.

If I played an even worse game of bridge than I usually do, perhaps it was because my whole attention was not on the game that evening. We were being offered an opportunity to buy something that could not be sold. After all, what value can be put on sunlight silences, deep clear water, the changing light on antique stone, the comfort of trees, the mysteries of fishing, on making love on the summer grasses of an island of your own?

I do not know how you can measure, in dollars, the taste of blueberries you gather, the darting flight of a swallow. There is no beauty or terror in money, but there is in a storm that comes to you freely, wonderful and frightening, the careless gift of a god. There is no monetary exchange that can assign a value to privacy or freedom. If you live with your wife and children on an island you own entirely, you govern as your own sovereign, free and competent to give your life whatever quality it will have. You can, on an island, teach your children many things more important than any they will ever learn in a city or a school. If you live on an island, the surrounding water is a moat defensive against the world when you need to be selfishly responsible to no one but yourself and your family, and there is no kind of money that can insulate you in the way that open, freely moving water can. Each of us needs something of an island in his life —if not an actual island, at least some place, or space in time, in which to be himself, free to cultivate his difference from others. Perhaps John Donne should have said that each man is an island but part of an archipelago.

We could not afford to buy the island. But neither could we afford not to buy the island. The island was important, and equally so were the great river, the countryside, and people who kept to a way of life that was at once more durable than and indifferent to the febrile and momentary concerns of an urban, cosmopolitan world. Who would not want an island, and what was money? I have always believed that money has no meaning until it is being spent; otherwise, it is a pile of wastepaper. If Bob wanted four thousand dollars for his island, I would give him four thousand dollars. The tactical problem of obtaining the money would no doubt be sorted out in due course.

Margaret and I never sat down, talked it out, and made a decision.

"It's like getting married" was all she ever said.

She said this the next day, apropos of nothing, as we made breakfast, but I followed her perfectly. As we so often did, we were each thinking of the same thing in our different ways. I had asked her to marry me the first evening I saw her. She had not immediately replied, except to say no as a matter of form, and I am sure we both knew what that meant. We were once again following a path toward a familiar but unknown destination.

2

Looking down from the Canadian span of the Thousand Islands Bridge in summertime, you have an aerial view of an extended marine version of the Hampton Court maze but one far more complicated than the royal garden's. Because the island trees are then in full leaf, many of the water paths are hidden even from your high vantage. Boats appear and disappear among the islands. The river channels are full, deep, and a Mediterranean blue in the sunlight of high summer. Here is one of the loveliest reaches of what may now be the last great North American river to remain reasonably clear and clean. Gamefish live in this river, and eagles wander over it.

In winter it is very different—as if the privet at

18

Hampton Court had been reduced to stumps to disclose the simple secret. The islands seem tiny steppingstones in a small, frozen creek. Everything has shrunk upon itself. You can see now the cottages that the leaves had concealed, all shuttered, their docks high out of water, the dock stavings like teeth in an old skull. It is difficult to imagine that anyone will ever live in those cottages again; it all looks as dead as an Andrew Wyeth painting.

One Indian legend says that the Thousand Islands of the St. Lawrence River were stones hurled by two warring gods—the Great Spirit, Manatoana, and the god of evil. They stood on either bank of the broad river, throwing masses of rock at each other. The stones that fell short landed in the water to become the islands. After Manatoana's victory, the Thousand Islands became variously known as the Garden Place or the Happy Hunting Ground of the Great Spirit. When Christianity came among the Indians, another story was told: When Eden was borne to Heaven by white-robed angels, a thousand flowers fell from the Garden and floated to the surface of the St. Lawrence to become the islands. Whichever legend most closely adheres to fact, both agree that the islands represented peace and divine beauty to the Indians.

Perhaps these aspects rather than common need led inimical tribes to preserve a kind of Peace of God when the eels were swarming off Grenadier Island. The Indian name for that island was Eel Fishing Ground, and there the tribes gathered in momentary amity to glut themselves on their wriggling catch. If you take a shovel and a sieve of stout wire and work up to your knees in muck among the rushes and the deer flies in the marshes at the foot of the island, you will find arrowheads, fishhooks, bits of pots, and stone tools of a great age. You may also find, from a more recent age, broken clay pipes and the rusted remains of Tower muskets. You can buy corn, garden vegetables, and live bait from the residents of this island, some of whom are descended from the red men who lost their arrowheads. Others are the latest heirs of the white men who dropped their pipes.

If you ignore the presence of summer cottages, or follow the twisting waterways at night when you can see only the dark bulk of islands standing in a moon path, you will see the region as the first Indians did. It is true that the giant oaks have gone, felled to become the ribs of Britain's battle line. Much heavier than water, the oak baulks had to be rafted down the river; and a well-preserved legend has it that a great pine raft, loaded with oak, broke up in a storm between McGoogan's Point and Rockport and that the oak is still down there in deep water, just as sound as the day it went into the river. If you fetched it up, the people say, the oak would rapidly decay. But if you kept it under water and used it as cribbing beneath boathouses, it would last forever. That there oak, they say, will be worth a lot of money to the man who finds her. So far no one has.

The great oaks are gone, but their descendants are now reaching an impressive size; and while the chestnuts perished in the blight and Dutch elm disease is slowly spreading in the region, the islands are as heavily wooded as once they were, and the *voyageurs,* if they returned today in their immense bark canoes loaded with beaver pelts, would see the stands of Lombardy poplars they set out. According to the story, the Frenchmen, exploring through the island maze, planted those trees to serve as guides to river channels, choosing Lombardy poplars not to remind themselves of home but because the European trees were strikingly different from the native ones and so could be readily identified.

However true that story is, a need to distinguish among the waterways must certainly have been a primary concern of the first explorers, as it remains today for anyone who cruises in the region. There are not a thousand islands. There are one thousand six hundred and ninety-seven of them, thickly strewn haphazardly in a fifty-mile stretch of the river that is twelve miles wide at the foot of Lake Ontario and gradually narrows to but two miles opposite the Canadian town of Brockville. You can, if you do not have a chart or a photographic memory, lose your way among the islands. You can, for instance, proceed up what seems to be a channel, only to find yourself locked into what proves to be an extensive backwater. There is a passage called Lost Channel, so named not because the channel was lost but because a British sloop of war was known to have entered it more than a hundred years ago, never to be seen again. No one knows what happened, nor where, in all the water paths, to look for whatever may be left of ship and crew.

In a curious way, the loss of that British sloop seems, like the warfare of the gods, to have occurred no longer ago than last week. When an aging lady tells you of her happy days as a young schoolteacher, when she and her pupils used to row nightly across the river during Prohibition, their skiffs laden with kegs of whisky to sell to thirsty Americans, it is obvious that she speaks from experience. But when she tells you about the time they burned the Jesuit missionary at a stake near what is now the third tee of the Grenadier Island Golf Club, you have the strange feeling that she remembers that, too. Just as the people of Sandwich, Kent, remember the visit of Elizabeth, in Rockport they remember that oak going down when the raft broke and the time they set fire to the missionary.

Twenty years ago I sensed that the local population of the Thousand Islands had this rather Indian view of time, in which the past merges into an enormous present, with tomorrow as distant as a star. They lived in time rather than using, wasting, spending, killing, or trying somehow to save time. I found this as appealing and as necessary to me as the natural beauty of the region, its aspects as a garden, and its legends. I wanted to live with them in time in their renewable garden. I was then at that vulnerable age when a man, arrived at last into possession of his powers, must decide how to live his life.

One man who was perfectly at home in the time continuum was our first, best friend on the river, William J. Slate. He looked after the Bodine property in winter, and in summers past Will had taught us where the fish were, how to catch and clean them, how to read the weather signs, and how to handle boats. He was a great believer in the therapeutic qualities of shellac, used as an ointment for open wounds, and Margaret and I went to visit him the morning after we looked at Bob's island. One of the virtues of a small community is that there are no secrets. We knew that Will would know why we had come and that he would tell us what we needed to know.

Will was rocking gently on the gray boards of his storm-windowed porch, looking across the Canadian channel to the cliffs where we had met David the day before. No one was on the river now. There was a snow sky, and the river was the color of the old polished steel in medieval armories. Margaret went inside to visit with Will's wife, Effie. Everything inside the house was for women, everything outside for men. The porch, even though it was enclosed for the winter, was outside the house and therefore a place for men to talk.

"She'll start to freeze now," Will promised. "I bet this year she'll freeze hard enough for you to drive a car right across her. There's a Ford on the bottom, just out there past Little Ninety-Nine. They thought the ice would hold, but she didn't."

"When was that?" I asked.

"Oh, gee, that was back in Mr. Weeks's time."

I drew up a wooden porch rocker for myself. It was polite and important to visit before coming to the point. In summers past, Margaret and I had often spent two hours and more visiting at inland farms in the course of buying a pound of butter or a dozen eggs. At first we used to ask straight out, "Do you have any butter today?" and the farm wife would say, "Well, I don't rightly know," and that was all we ever learned until a signal, usually in the form of a question, was given for us to leave: "Would you folks like some butter today?" Thereafter, we always chatted, never stating the object of our call until the question was asked, and in time the conver-

23

sation—not the butter—became the object of our visit for us as well as for the farm wife.

"How did you first meet Mr. Weeks?" I asked Will, because I was curious to know.

"Oh, by gee, that was something," Will said. "I was on a pebble scow. We was going upriver to Darling's with a load of gravel to put in behind their dock, and old Mr. Weeks was standing up in his boat waving his hat. He was drifting down on that point, and he saw me and hollered, 'Hey, young feller, can you start my boat?' and I said to him, 'Well, yes, I think I can.'

"We came alongside in the scow, and I got in her and he'd flooded her was all. It was one of the engines that old Huck made down to his shop. I gave the petcocks a turn, set the spark, got a good hold of the flywheel and gave her a spin, and she started right up as nice as you please. Old Mr. Weeks he looked at me and said, 'You don't want to spend the rest of your life on that scow, do you?' and I said no, I guessed I didn't care if I did, and he said, 'All right, young feller, from now on you're working for me.'

"Oh," Will said, "we had great times in those days."

"Tchk," I said, in the Canadian sound of wonder.

We rocked together. Will was a wiry, straight-backed old man who looked like a Chelsea pensioner with a good bit of American Indian in him. He was, in fact, part Indian, the rest Scots-Irish, and he had been born in a cabin a few hundred yards downriver. The great days of the great times had occurred when the century was young, when there had been many more sailboats than naphtha boats on the river and more naphtha boats than those with the new home-made gasoline engines. In those days, you most probably sailed, if you did not row in pursuit of your lawful occasions, and if you were invited to tea upriver, you had to estimate the winds and currents in order to arrive at four. Maids in black uniforms with little white explosions on their heads and little white aprons served tea to the ladies on the lawn, while the gentlemen had whisky in the library. For the gentry at teatime, the indoor-outdoor order of things was apparently reversed. I had seen the yellowing photographs.

Will, wearing a chauffeur's uniform, polished boots and cap and a somewhat Celtic grin, had been old Mr. Weeks's boatman then. In overalls, looking more Indian, Will had been the fishing guide, carpenter, plumber, stonemason, mechanic, gardener, house painter, and lawn mower for the house and land that Mr. Weeks had bought on the Canadian riverbank. Will was no longer a boatman, for with one antique female exception, no one on the river now kept the sort of stately mahogany launch, glittering with brass brightwork, that should be piloted only by a servant in livery. You could see that Will missed all that.

"He was one of the rich pots who used to come here for the summer," Will wanted me to know. "He had a solid gold pass that let him go free on any railroad or steamship line in the world, but he never went anywhere. He always came here instead. He said there wasn't anywhere else like this."

"No," I said, "there isn't."

"Ehup," Will agreed.

Then, rocking on his porch, Will told me what, as the new member of the family, I ought to know. Old Mr. Weeks, who was Margaret's and Bob's grandfather, had run away from a farm near Buffalo as a semiliterate boy to become a telegrapher, then a passenger agent, and ultimately a big pot on the Reading Railroad. Then he had a train of his own and could go anywhere in the world but always came to the river instead to have great times with Will.

"He had a Palace Car and a baggage car all to himself for him and the family," Will said. "He'd leave the cars at Redwood, and they'd take the trolley to the Bay, and I'd meet them at the Bay and fetch them over here."

Will referred to the New York town of Alexandria Bay, some five miles across the river opposite the village of Rockport. I had heard about the trolley before. It ran through seven miles of open country, and when winter came gangs of men had to hand-shovel the line clear of snow that drifted higher than their heads. Because the trolley ran on electricity, there was a power line from Redwood to the Bay, and because there was no reason to keep the power on after the last trolley run in the evening, there was no electricity in the Bay at night.

My brother-in-law Bob was old enough to remember that trolley ride, although Margaret was not. The family trip to Canada from Philadelphia began in February, Bob had told me, when the great steamer trunks were packed with all that everyone would need in summer and sent ahead. For the children who watched their toy sailboats and other treasures disappear into the trunks, the promise that they could have them again in

Canada was never completely satisfactory. Then in late spring the rest of the trip began. The touring cars would take the grandmother, the mother, the four children, the two Irish maids, and the colored laundress to Wayne Junction, where an officer of the Reading Railroad would see them safely into the Palace Car. At Hoboken another would see them onto the ferry and across the Hudson to New York and Grand Central Station, where he put them on the overnight train to Redwood. The train arrived there in the early morning, and the trolley took them to the depot at Alexandria Bay, where at dockside they would find the steamer trunks in a shed and Will waiting in his boatman's costume to hand them into the long-bowed mahogany family launch with its bright brass ventilating funnels and its wicker chairs. Will had heard of colored people, but he had never seen one before that laundress appeared, and as soon as he got the chance he took her down to the river and gave her a bar of laundry soap to see if she could wash off the black. He meant it as a joke, and perhaps in that innocent time it was—at least for Will.

Later in the summer, when they had assured themselves that their corporate empires could survive their brief absences, gentlemen from New York who had summer cottages in the Thousand Islands would arrive with cigars in their mouths and bourbon on their breaths to rejoin their ladies and children. There were polo matches at the Thousand Islands Club, auction bridge in the evenings, and a fair amount of entertaining in the tremendous frame houses the summer people called cottages. Paris Singer, the sewing-machine man, built a stone castle you can still see downriver, on Dark Island, and George Boldt, owner of the Waldorf-Astoria, built an even grander one on an island directly in front of Alexandria Bay. Pullman, the Palace Car builder, had a cottage on an island near Boldt's Castle; Grover Cleveland stayed at the Crossman House Hotel, and for a while it seemed that the whole world came to the Bay. Tiffany's opened a branch there, and provision ships came upriver from Montreal laden with French wines and filets of beef. Few of the summer people swam in the river. They might go down to the water's edge, tiptoe in among the stones in their bathing shoes and long bathing skirts—the men's bathing suits brightly striped and daringly exposing hairy forearms and calves—and dribble a bit of water on themselves. The men, grinning and laughing, would splash the appropriately timid and twittering ladies, and everyone had a bully time, but few of them could swim. Swimming was not the major sport. Fishing was.

"We used to get some dandy fish," Will said, "and a guide would get three dollars a day. He'd supply the boat, the bait, the fish rods, the steak, corn, potatoes, some bacon to get the pan ready for the fish, the flour to fry them in, and two kinds of berry pie and coffee for lunch. If you was a guide, you'd row them thirty miles a day. You'd start out upriver, and at midday you'd find an island where you'd go ashore to clean their fish and make a fire and fix their lunch and have a shore dinner. Then you'd fish downriver again, with the wind and the current. You'd make three times what most fellows made a day, and of course you had the fishing, too."

In those days of great financial rewards, Mr. Weeks had once given Will a raise. Will promptly bought a trotting horse that never won a race. He never got another raise. Old Mr. Weeks gave him coal for the winter instead. The Reading, I remembered, was a coal-carrying railroad.

"Now those boats," Will said, "they should never have left that island."

He looked at me closely, with his flat Indian look, and it was a moment before I understood he was no longer talking about the skiffs of the fishing guides in the days of the great times. The visit was over, and serious discussion was at hand. Will had re-entered the year 1952, and the boats to which he referred were those that Bob had acquired with the island.

"You'll need a boat," Will told me, assuming that we would of course be buying Bob's island, for otherwise we would not have come all the way from Maryland to spend a weekend out of season.

"Bob said if we bought the island he'd throw in the old sailboat you made over into an outboard," I said.

Will drew in his breath in that Canadian way that implies the acceptance of fate. He looked more Indian than ever.

"You'll need another one," he said. "Nobody can be on an island with one boat. Suppose you're chopping wood, and you cut your leg with the ax and the engine won't start."

"Do you know where we can get a skiff?"

I was thinking of one of those lovely, light-on-the-water, double-ended St. Lawrence skiffs made of lapped cedar strakes.

"Oh, gee, there's a lot of wind out there," Will said.

"But you can take a skiff out in anything, and you never have engine trouble."

"Yes, and you can row an hour right beside the same rock in some winds, too," Will said.

I rocked in obedience to local authority.

"That there's a hawk," Will said.

We had both been watching the slow circles above the Club Island cliffs.

"A hawk in winter?"

"I don't know about that," Will said, "but that there's a hawk."

So it was.

"Now, you ought to have an inboard like the one Robert got with the island," Will said. "Not the Gar Wood; she's got a Vee bottom. Oh, she'll go fast, but she'll pound. You want a round bottom, like the one with the cabin has. Now that boat, she should never have left her."

"Would you want to help us look for a boat?" I asked.

"Well, yes, I think I would," Will said.

With that, the old man left his chair to ask Effie if there was any coffee. Margaret had been helping Effie prepare coffee and sandwiches. It was time for us to join the ladies in their realm and allow them to serve us, now that we lordly men had visited each other and discussed matters of importance that women would never understand. Will told them that we would go looking at boats after lunch. Margaret wanted to come, too. Will looked a bit surprised, but he said he guessed she could. I supposed the rules of etiquette did not apply to her, not because she was old Mr. Weeks's granddaughter but because Will still thought of her as a child he had taught to swim. I had no idea what Will thought of me. I felt like a hawk out of season.

3

The distance between Canada and the United States is much wider than the St. Lawrence River which forms the boundary, and the Thousand Islands Bridge connects the two nations by leaps of the imagination. The Bridge, as everyone calls it, is actually four bridges. To leave Canada you take a running start, then soar over the arc of a suspension span, alight, hop over a girder bridge, run a bit past the Canadian Customs House, skip over a small masonry arch, and walk to the United States Customs House. Here you have an opportunity to catch your breath. Then you run for eight miles across Wellesley Island, which, because of its rocks and trees, still looks exactly like Canada. But the ground suddenly falls away from beneath you, and you soar up and away in another suspended arc to land beside a filling station.

You are now definitely in another country. Instead of forests there are flat farm fields with billboards strung out on them.

We went with Will to look for a boat in Alexandria Bay, New York, because he said they had some dandy ones there and, I gathered, because they had places over there where you could buy a drink. I gathered this from Effie's suspicious look when Will said we'd go to the Bay. We drove across the Bridge because it was far too cold to cross the river in an open boat. It was too cold for snow. The sky kept darkening, but the clouds seemed to have congealed, and beneath the blue-black sky was that kind of windless, empty, bottomless cold that gives you frostbite if you remain long out of doors. There were no other automobiles on the Bridge nor on the road that led through the billboards to the Bay.

There was no one on the town's streets, but we found men in the boatyard doing winter work. The boat-yard was one of the Bay's two sources of income in winter. The other one, according to the president of the Bay's bank, was the state unemployment compensation office. The men in the boatyard were heavy-bodied and middle-aged, dressed in oil-stained dark trousers, old sweatshirts, and open Mackinaws. They were sitting close to a potbellied iron stove, drinking coffee poured from a pot on the stove lid, talking slowly and smoking. They looked up as we came in, and they said hello to Will. They nodded to us. One of them told Will we could look around; the door to the shed wasn't locked.

33

Now, there is something about looking at boats, particularly if you know nothing about them and do not intend to buy one, that brings out the blue-water sailorman in you. You enter a world of chines and knees, strakes and keelsons; you thump a hull and nod as if you understood what a stuffing box was—and there you are, rounding the Horn in a full gale, driving the lee rail under as, with a marlin spike in each fist, you dominate a terrified and mutinous crew of gin-crazed Lascars.

Or you become the wealthy yachtsman. Cost means nothing to you. With fine contempt, you dismiss the broker's ridiculous suggestion that the $65,000 cruiser he shows you could possibly suit your needs. You do not want a stinkpot; you are a sailorman. You feel he should know that you, in your J boat, raised the Lizard a good two weeks ahead of the pack from Newport.

In my time, I have variously been Lightning Johnny of the China tea trade, skipper of the fastest clipper ever to leave the Baltimore yards, and Vice Admiral of the Blue Sir John of the Royal Yacht Squadron, whenever I looked at boats. But on that day with Will and Margaret the magic was absent. A fact, as cold as the day itself, was that we would have to buy a boat. We were not going to look at boats. We were going to buy one. If you had an island, you had to have a boat. We could see our breaths in the gloom of the shed, and I could not imagine any of the boats in the water. Up on timbers for the winter, full of dust, bits of weeds and dead leaves, were hulks with flaking decks, missing seats, rotten ropes, broken floorboards, ancient engines, and suspicious hulls.

34

Will looked upon this debris with a steady eye, pointing out the valuable differences.

"Now that there is the kind you want," he would say whenever we stared at a particularly loathsome wreck. "You want a good sea boat like that one there, with a round bottom, because a round-bottom boat will go through a sea as nice as you please, or if you're coming across the wind, you can slow her down and roll right with her and never get a drop of water on you."

The boats he particularly admired were the long, round-hulled workboats with inboard engines, but very few of these were for sale. They were the property of rivermen, not summer people, and those that were for sale were, apparently, those that even the local people felt were not worth trying to repair. Nonetheless, the asking prices of the wrecks were nearly half what Bob wanted for his island.

We made our way around the derelicts, the pendant chain falls, the eviscerated engine blocks on the shed's planked floor, and out into the somewhat brighter gloom of the freezing day. The grass was brittle underfoot. Ice was thickening near the stones at water's edge, and the river buoys that had been pulled high on the shore lay stranded on the frozen grass like rusting carcasses of metal dinosaurs. Seen from the shore, against the heavy sky, Boldt's Castle seemed more forlorn than ever. We could see the stone chamois cold and lonely atop one steep roof of the castle that George built.

"Would you like some coffee?" I asked Will.

Yes, he said, he would—and he knew of a bar where we could get some.

"You just have to keep looking," Will told us as he sipped at his whisky. He had ordered whisky because, he said, he'd just remembered the coffee at this bar was terrible. So we all had whisky.

"Anyway," he said, "that's the kind you'd want if I was you. They want a terrible price, but if you keep looking, you'll find one. Maybe Chub will have a boat for you, or Chuckie."

He referred to two of his wife's great-nephews. Chub Massey was a fishing guide and proprietor of a tourist camp; Chuck Handley was a truck driver who had an island on the river, a cabin cruiser, and four speedboats.

"He got every one of them from off the bottom of the river," Will told us. "Chuckie would ask the owner if he wanted him to dive her up, or what the fellow wanted for her now she was stove in and on the bottom, and one of them he got for nothing. He'd dive her up and him and his boy Stevie would work on her all winter, and in the spring he'd have her all just like new. Or now Chub, he might know of a boat."

Chub's tourist camp was on Wellesley Island, just off the road that led from the the American span of the bridge to the United States Customs House, and Will suggested we stop in on our way back. We paid for the whisky and left to walk down what had once been a village street not without charm and what was now a strip of hoagie stands and bars, boarded up for winter.

"Oh, gee," Will said, "they used to have wonderful places here."

"Back in the days when Boldt was building his castle?"

"Why yes," he said as we got in the car. "Just think of that. Buying that island and making it into a heart."

I could imagine it very well. Poor George, the German dishwasher. He had dreamed of living with his bride in a castle on the Rhine. Unfortunately, he could not earn enough money by washing dishes in Germany to afford a Rhenish castle, so he came to America to wash dishes. He wound up owning the Waldorf-Astoria, the perfect American immigrant success story. Then George Boldt built his castle. He had an island shaped in the form of a heart, as Will said, and called it Heart Island, and on this he had a Rhenish castle built as a valentine to the woman who, to him, would always be his bride.

"Oh, that was something," Will said. "We must have broke more than two thousand yards of stone."

"You did?"

"Oh, yes. I guess there wasn't a fellow on either side of the river that didn't work on that castle, or on them canals and the boathouses. I don't know what Mr. Boldt thought. Maybe he thought you had to keep a ship indoors at night or when it rains. Anyway, you've seen those boathouses, how the doors open up all the way to the top so the masts can go in? I never heard of a boathouse for a full-rigged ship before, but Mr. Boldt, he wanted them, so we built them."

George Boldt had wanted many things. Those canals were carved out of an island adjacent to Heart Island, and Boldt, envisioning summer nights when he, his bride, and their guests would float along moonlit waterways, imported gondolas from Venice, together with gondoliers. Great crates of stone sculpture also arrived from Italy, as did Italian stonemasons. He had a watergate built in the form of a triumphal arch to lead his guests into the heart of his island kingdom. It was here, while George Boldt watched the construction from his yacht, that he was served a salad with a different dressing. He wondered what it was, and the yacht's chef, thinking quickly, said Thousand Island Dressing. George was so pleased that he immediately promoted the fellow to the rank of chef at his New York hotel, where for years he reigned as Oscar of the Waldorf.

"I remember just as clear as anything when that telegram came," Will said. "And everything stopped just as it was. The telegram said Mrs. Boldt had died and everybody was fired."

"So *that's* why the castle was never finished?"

"Yes," Will said. "That's why. Mr. Boldt, he never came back to the river again."

So that was the end of one version of the American dream.

No guests ever passed beneath that triumphal arch. No gondolas ever moved along those canals, whose stone banks are now crumbling. The sculpture, Will said, was still in its crates. One of the Alexandria Bay tour boat lines bought the boathouses and the castle. Tour boats, not full-rigged ships, are stored in the boathouses in winter. The only people to visit the castle are tourists who file through the empty rooms in summer and leave their names in lipstick on the walls. In winter, snow blows through the paneless bedroom windows and drifts across the warping floor of the ballroom where no one ever danced.

The once opulent cottages of the millionaires are, for the most part, more ruined than the castle. Some have been pulled down; others have suffered the possibly worse fate of becoming small hotels. Where Tiffany's had been, there was, for a while, a shop that sold sneezing powder and pillows that made a rude noise when you sat on them. The Pullman house disappeared. No one plays polo at the Thousand Islands Club, which is no longer a club but a commercial hotel. No one on the river knows just why fashion left the Thousand Islands. Some say a way of life ended when the income-tax laws were passed; others say the stock-market crash in 1929 ended it. Another theory is that the automobile and airplane put an end to going to just one place in summer. One man supposed it was because the servants disappeared. And a good thing, too, he went on to say, because no one should be another man's servant. I thought of his remark as we drove with Will through the winter ghost that was the Bay. It occurred to me that the more free a man might be from pride and arrogance and the more certain of himself, the less likely he is to believe in democracy. Will had no use for democracy.

We returned past the filling stations and the billboards to the bridge. Certain animals and birds are found only in certain habitats or in specific kinds of dwelling places. If you build a wren house, then wrens —and only wrens—will find it and move in. If you build motels and put up pizza stands and gas pumps anywhere in the world, tourists—and only tourists—will find them and move in. No one knows where they come from or where they go when they leave. But tourists were what the Bay had now instead of millionaires. They would begin to appear when the mosquitoes were biting: a curious swarm of curiously dressed people of no definable origin or fixed address, whose annual migration through the region in summer helped to create a local unemployment problem in winter.

Chub Massey's camp lay just inside the United States, or just outside Canada, depending on how you looked at it. He was an American who was a member of a Canadian family, but he spent most of his summer in neither country, for he was a fishing guide and spent that time on the water. He was so popular that by April all of his summer days were reserved by people who wanted to catch bass. The little cabins that Chub had built did not attract nomadic tourists but men who came largely from northern Pennsylvania, where they kept small businesses in small towns. It was their principal pleasure to get away from their wives and children for a week or so, to escape to a masculine world where they could tell each other locker-room lies, drink whisky, and catch bass. The cabins were shuttered when we drove up to them, but Chub was there, preparing his boathouse for the winter. It was easy to see how he came by his name. Will introduced us, and we visited a while in the local fashion, which consists of making true statements about the weather, people, and recent phenomena, each statement followed by a cogent silence while its truth is assessed, proved, and digested. At length Will said we were looking for a boat. That was a truth that bore considerable thought.

"Well," Chub said after thinking about this, "would you want to see one?"

Actually, he showed us two. Each was fourteen feet long. He was particularly proud of the first, which he had built and called the Pancake because it was so low and wide. But, he said, with a ten-horse on her, she'd plane right along like a race boat. The other was a routine factory plywood hull with a modified Vee bottom. Put a ten-horse on her, he said, and she'd zip right along, too. Since we were summer people, Chub presumed we were interested in speed. We could try them out if we wanted. It wouldn't take a minute to put them in the water.

An hour later we were glad to be back in the car with its heater. It had been stunningly cold, speeding around the freezing river; we had done this for only a very few minutes in each boat. The Pancake leaked and needed work done; the second boat seemed better to me, but Will cautioned us against plywood. After a while, he said, the water would get to her and she'd come unglued. Chub would sell us either one for the same price. For little more than $400 he would give us a used boat and a used outboard motor. We said we would think it over.

"Gee, I don't know," Will said as we drove on, re-crossing the border into Canada. "If you got the time, JK, you could look down to Andress'. He might have something for you."

"It's four-thirty," I said.

"Oh, he'll be there," Will said.

It is two miles from the Bridge to Rockport, and you might very well never see the village if you were not looking for the road that turns off the highway toward the river. The wooden gate that welcomes you into Rockport is invisible until you have either passed it at fifty miles an hour or, knowing where the turn is, left the highway to pass beneath it. You cannot see the village from the highway because it lies behind a screen of trees

41

and runs steeply downhill to the water. The village's one brick house stands at the top of the hill, just inside the gate, and across from this is the small, brown-shingled Anglican church. Farther down the hill, but built on a rock commanding a view of the river, is the white-painted Catholic church. Otherwise, the village consists of one street, a few frame houses, two stores, a town dock and a customs dock, and three marine businesses. The oldest and at that time the largest of these businesses was carried on in a single boathouse whose sign read "W. E. Andress & Son," and over the door was a smaller sign that said "Post Office."

Ed Andress was a green old man, the postmaster of Rockport, proprietor of its gasoline pump, and a builder of docks, summer houses, and boats and who, in the course of a long career, had lost several fingers to buzz saws. We found him in his bib overalls peering through his spectacles at a tray of copper rivets of mixed sizes and standing ankle deep in the sawdust of his cedar-scented workshop where men were making skiffs. A wood-fired iron stove heated water to a boil, sending the steam through a long stove pipe; one of the workmen was drawing a thin and supple cedar board from the open and steaming end of this pipe as we arrived. The hot wet cedar was then bent into the several curves it had to assume to become one of the lapstrakes of the boat taking form upon a jig. Bent, it was riveted into place.

"You used to be able to buy one for twenty-five dollars, but I don't know," Ed Andress said. "I don't know what fellows think any more. Why, now, the way people think, everybody has to have money. In that skiff

42

there you'll have three hundred dollars just in the wood and the copper, never mind the wages, before you can sell her, and there just isn't the same cedar any more."

He was one of the last men still building St. Lawrence skiffs, using design and methods more than a hundred years old. Once everyone had skiffs, and Ed loved to build and varnish them, but as he said, nobody wanted them any more—everyone wanted to go fast instead. There was no more demand for the four-oared skiffs, or for the sailing skiffs; people wanted outboard motorboats. He was building this one because he wanted to build it, although it would take him a time to sell it. He thought one of the rich summer people might want it. He did not refer to the vanished millionaires but to the newly rich automobile salesmen who felt a need for antiques and portraits of other people's ancestors. Ed was building a new antique and he was not entirely happy, despite the comfort it gave him. He was willing to sell this one for fifty dollars more than it cost to build, but it was a price that a General Motors accountant might find uneconomical in view of the time it would take Ed to build it. His time, the accountant would say, could have been more profitably used making something most people would buy—such as making outboard motorboat hulls out of sheets of painted plywood.

The old man did not have a boat for us, although he said he would keep looking. Nor would he agree to help us repair the broken dock, the stairs and roof, or otherwise look after the island as he did for others. He said he would like to help, but he already had more to do than he could get to, especially with the way it was now with men taking jobs in town instead of working for him on the river. He suggested we see Ed Huck, because Ed was just starting up and had four sons.

It was dark and late in the afternoon but bright and warm in the combined machine shop and boathouse whose sign said "Ed Huck Marine Ltd." Like Will and Ed Andress and almost everyone else in the Rockport community, Ed Huck was a plumber, carpenter, boatwright, and mechanic. He was a short, thick, powerfully built man with a great blade of a nose. He was younger than Will, but he had been a boatman for a wealthy Canadian family, a rumrunner during Prohibition, then a taxicab driver in Montreal. Now he and his four sons were operating the small boatyard that had been his father's. We found him in a pool of light, using a power drill to bore holes in hull planks. He used a power screwdriver to set the screws. He was making outboard motorboats to rent to fishermen who would come to stay in the cabins he had built on a lawn beside his boathouse. Yes, he said, over the shriek of his power drill, he'd be glad to help us.

"And by Jesus," he said, "the first thing you want to do is get rid of that goddam kerosene before you burn the house down."

"Oh, you know the island, then?" I asked.

"I been there a hundred times," he said. "I put the electricity in her."

He shut off the power drill and looked at us.

"What you might better do, JK, is put in bottle gas," he said. "You might better get yourself a gas fridge, a stove, and a hot-water heater over to the States, because

44

they'll be a hell of a lot cheaper there than they are for the same thing over here."

He told us that we could bring everything we needed without paying Canadian customs duties on it, if we brought it all across the Bridge at once, as Settlers First Effects. After that, he said, we would have to pay duty on any other manufactured goods we brought into Canada. I told him I guessed that we would not be able to take advantage of the settlers' exemption, because we could not possibly afford to buy, all at once, everything we would need.

"Then fetch it over at night," he said.

He told us of a boathouse on Wellesley Island where everybody left his things before going through Canadian customs.

"Nobody will bother your stuff," he said, "because everybody leaves his stuff there. That boathouse is full of things—radios, stoves, dishwashers, anything you want. Just put yours there, and when it's dark, come back in a boat and fetch her over."

That water maze under the Bridge could not, I thought, have been more happily designed for criminal purposes. But Ed was not giving us criminal advice.

"Look, JK," he said, "if you was to bring the whole lot over, all at once, you'd pay no duty, hey? All right, now if you was to bring the same lot over, one thing at a time, you'd get the first one through, but you'd have to pay on all the others. Now you tell me what's the sense in that."

Like almost everyone else, Ed Huck was a reasonably honorable man. It made no sense to him to obey fool

45

regulations. I remembered that when one of the local men had become a game warden, it was said that "he went over to the other side." The people who said this did not mean he had deserted to the side of law and order. Rather, he had joined "them." The universal enemy of mankind is always that anonymous "they" or "them" who, by their fatuities, needlessly complicate ordinary lives. It is the fools in government, in any government, who always make trouble with their fool rules. Thus, to smuggle was no crime. It was simply to do in one way something that the law said you had to do in another. Since what you did amounted to the same thing, no matter which way you did it, why worry about what "they" thought of it? "Especially," Ed said, "when you got a right to." He spat, and "they" disappeared.

No, he said, he didn't have a boat for us. He needed for himself all the boats he could build. But he would keep his eyes and ears open. We could talk about it later.

"We're going to play Five Hundred tonight, Bill?" he asked Will Slate.

"Why, yes," Will said. "Down to your house."

"Well, if JK and Margaret was to come we could play six-handed, hey? Call for the ace you want, and that's your partner?"

The two men grinned at each other.

"We can have a game and talk about what you'll need, JK," Ed Huck said.

He switched on his power drill and said goodbye as he went on with his winter work, making what he needed against the time the ice would leave and the first fishermen would return.

46

That night we sat around a table in an overheated room—the Canadians keep their houses almost as warm as Eskimos keep their igloos—the men in shirt sleeves, the women in wash dresses, all of us drinking ale, playing cards and talking. Cassie Huck, Ed's wife, was a large, handsome woman who took a deep pleasure in constant hard work and who had little good to say for anyone who, by her standards, was lazy. She was the proprietor, cook, and manager of the tourist side of the Huck enterprise; she looked after the cabins Ed had built and cooked for the fishermen who rented them. Will's wife Effie was a winter apple of a woman with white hair and sharp little eyes. She had seven married sons, the first six by a prior husband. She was a midwife, made a wonderful pie crust, and could drive nails with her single-shot .22-caliber rifle. She shot snakes with it and once brought down a Canada goose with a shot through the head. Effie was a past noble grand of the Rebeccas; Cassie, a twenty-five-year jewel of the Eastern Star; Will was a Rebecca; and Ed, a chartered Mason. The lodges formed a great part of their winter lives, the men meeting in their mysteries and the women in theirs.

Ed told about the time Will got drunk in Alexandria Bay and dived off the dock and everyone spent most of the night looking for him in the water. When they eventually returned to Rockport, convinced they had done all they could and that they would have to grapple for him in the morning, they found Will sitting in his wet clothes on the Rockport dock, saying, "What kept you so long?"

"Drink," Effie rather bleakly said, "always was his failing."

Everyone laughed, and it was not till later that you realized Will had swum for five miles in his clothes that night.

During the game I was frequently Will's partner, and I discovered that, whatever his failings may have been, bidding was not one of them. He was a daring and accurate bidder. He seemed to know what was in my hand as well as I did. He kept looking at a spot somewhere over my head while making up his mind what to bid, and it eventually dawned on me that I was sitting directly beneath a large mirror. Thereafter, I fanned the cards out to give him a good look at them, not so much to cheat but for the fun of watching Will peering at the mirror. It was even more fun to fold the cards quickly together and watch Will's eyes drop and move sideways, trying now to see in other people's hands. Meanwhile, there were stories. Effie told about the snowy night when their son Edson (named for old Mr. Weeks) saw a black bear in the light of his car's headlamps just as he turned off the road to come down the lane to Will's house. Edson slid to a stop, jumped out, reached under the seat for a tire iron, and went blundering into the snow in the dark, determined to brain a bear. The trouble was, she said, the bear got away. Everyone felt this was too bad, because a bearskin rug would have been just dandy.

Yes, Cassie said, she remembered that year; that was a great year for bears. It was a cold winter and they came right to the village for garbage. Now they were getting more timber wolves, Ed said, and the Slates agreed. I gathered from the description that these were not those great-shouldered and head-swaying gray ghosts you can still see in the northwestern wilderness but rather were coyotes, and the feral mixture of coyotes and farm strays, that sometimes killed calves. The coyotes, it seemed, were slowly moving in from the west, and there was a bounty on them. Several had been shot on Grenadier, Grindstone, and the larger islands, as well as in the wood-lots of farms behind Rockport.

That reminded Effie about the time the sleigh over-turned and the horse ran away. She and Will had been going down to visit on Grenadier Island, she said, with the trotter stepping right out and the sleigh skidding around on the river ice, buffeted by a cross wind. Then all of a sudden over we went, she said, and there we was, upside down, sliding along in the snow with Will sawing on the reins, trying to stop a runaway horse. My, she said, that was something. When he got the horse stopped, our clothes was full of snow, she said, just packed tight with it, and she was afraid they'd freeze to death. But Will just told her to take her clothes off and shake them out, and that is what they did. They stripped naked, out there on the ice, shook their clothing free of snow, dressed—and continued on their way to what Effie said was a lovely visit with Minnie Buell.

I cannot recall that we ever talked that night about what we would need for the island, as Ed had suggested we might. I do remember the talk was about the river in winter. From bears and wolves and horses and ice the talk went on to ducks and deer, and there was almost nothing that Margaret and I could add to this. It was not precisely our fault; the problem was that our experiences were irrelevant or unexceptional. We could tell about delivering our second child at home when she arrived before there was time to drive to the hospital or summon a physician, but this would hardly be impressive to Effie and not much more so to Will and the Hucks. They all took an ominous view of hospitals and a somewhat suspicious one of physicians, and belonged to a community that had many, if not most, of its children at home. Nor could I say much about my work, when asked about it, because my work consisted of looking at what other people did rather than doing anything myself, and the things that a Washington newspaperman looked at were of very little interest to residents of a small Canadian village. But then we were under no obligation to add to the stories. We obviously enjoyed them, and the Slates and the Hucks were glad to have an audience and an opportunity to live over the impressive occasions of their lives. At midnight Cassie brought out what they called a lunch of sandwiches, cakes, pies and coffee, and it was nearly two in the morning before we said good night.

During that long winter weekend when we looked at an island and looked for a boat, the region seemed cold, shrunken, and remote from a larger world. But a warmth beat at the heart of it. We learned there were barn dances on Saturday nights, and sometimes there would be lovely fights that were treasured in memory. They were a lot better, Effie said, "than the wrestling you see at the arena." Motion pictures had no place, it seemed, in winter evenings. No one talked about them, although they did talk about going to the hockey matches and watching the curling in Gananoque, where Scots in kilts and tams sent the stones trundling down the ice, the sweepers brooming away before the rumbling stones, and everyone holding his breath. During the long winter nights the village women and their daughters met at quilting bees to sew and gossip in one room while their men drank ale and gossiped in another, and at midnight they would all have the kind of lunch that Cassie had set out for us. Birthdays, anniversaries, and funerals were great occasions. It occurred to me that, if the people did not go to motion pictures, the reason might be that they preferred living their own lives to looking at pictures of improbably beautiful people acting out equally improbable nonsense.

Here on the Ontario riverbank lived a people variously descended from Indians, a *voyageur* or two, British soldiers, Highlanders, and fugitives from the American Revolution, all wanderers in a wilderness who had paused beside the river and remained to cut timber, quarry stone, fish, trap, and farm. Excitements had come and gone: the Indian wars, the Revolution, the War of 1812 (which took the form of bucolic skirmishes and cattle raids as well as of more impressive demonstrations of the military science), the appearance of paddle-wheel steamships. The arrival of the millionaires had been exciting. Then there had been the First World War. Boys from both banks of the river had gone to that, the Canadian boys going first, called in the names of honor, duty, glory, leaving the silences of the great river, the smell of sun-warmed pines, and the ripples made by a leaping bass, for the unceasing noise and grotesque horrors. The names of Rockport's dead, buried in

France, were placed on a memorial by the riverbank.

For a time virtually every adult and many a child on either side of the river was involved in some way in the care and feeding of the millionaires in summer, but however lucrative this may have been, evidently it had little to do with the basic stuff of river life, for when the millionaires disappeared after the First World War, departing as inexplicably as they had come, the local populace managed to survive without them. Prohibition in America provided money and entertainment for everyone until the gangsters arrived from the cities and the shooting began. At this point the river people gave up playing hide and seek at night on the river with the United States border patrols and abandoned the field to the gangsters. The Great Depression meant hard times on the river, but not so catastrophically hard as those felt in the urban world, for a man on the river could keep a cow, while the man in the city apartment could not. The only thing that went out of river life was money, and although that loss was certainly felt, it did not also mean the loss of morale, self-respect, and position that accompanies loss of money in the city.

This was made clear to us by a friend we met that weekend. During the eight weeks of July and August that comprised the tourist season, our friend had grossed $300 as a fishing guide. Now, in 1952, there was no depression but rather a general prosperity. Still, $300 was what he had earned, and he and his wife and children left their home-made trailer to live on a summer resident's houseboat that had been beached for the winter. He had tapped the public power line for heat and light, and, by gee, he said, that made it nice and cozy. They were surviving the winter largely on a barrel of lard, two hundred pounds of potatoes, and fish he illegally netted. When the river froze, he would fish through the ice. If some well-intentioned soul with a government job and a head full of theory had paid that family an official visit and certified them for public housing and a dole, our friend would have been insulted and demeaned. He did not think of himself as poor, nor did anyone else. He was just having a run of bad luck, everyone agreed. Sometimes you have good luck and sometimes you have bad luck, and if some folks had a lot of money, that was lucky for them, but it did not mean they were better than anyone else in the ways that really counted. But if you went up to a man and told him that his house wasn't good enough for you and that he didn't earn enough to please you, you might as well have just gone up to him and knocked him down, kicked him, and walked over him.

The area is not and never was an aquatic Shangri-La populated by rugged individuals uninterested in and undisturbed by what is happening in the wider world. (Hitler had his effect: new names were added to the war memorials.) Yet most of the people can take care of themselves better than city people can, and many of our technological advances serve them more as diversions that necessities. The invention of the internal combustion engine is one example. More than seventy-five thousand communities in the United States now absolutely depend on that engine for their very existence. While the river people certainly find the engine useful, if it were suddenly to disappear, the horse, sails, and oars could replace it at very little cost, if any, to the basic quality of river life. Similarly, if electricity disappeared, Rockport could survive without it, just as it survived the disappearance of the millionaires. The simpler life of the river people makes them better candidates for survival. As Neutra said, the specialist is the gravedigger of society, and the urban world consists almost entirely of specialists. An entire community can dig its own grave through specialization, too. You could see what specializing in the tourist trade had already done to the Bay, and I hoped that the people in Rockport would not make the same mistake and would continue to embrace change without being particularly affected by it. I supposed that some would and that others would not, for not a few of Rockport's young looked to the city.

As far as Margaret and I were concerned, all that we knew from summers past, together with all that we saw, heard, and felt on that winter weekend, made us look to the river and led us to tell her brother that we would buy his island.

We were unable to find the kind of boat we wanted and needed at a price we could afford, but now, if ever, was the time to buy, for the prices would go up in the spring. In the end we gave Chub a deposit on the plywood boat.

Ed Huck told us what it would cost to repair the boathouse and its dock and to replace the dangerous, kerosene-operated appliances. He suggested a contractor who could do the work cheaply and well and where

54

on the American side of the river we might look for bottle-gas appliances. We could not make the underwater repairs ourselves, he said, because that was winter work and we would not be in Rockport during the winter. You had to wait, he said, till the river went down far enough to expose the damaged cribbing, and then wait until the water froze so that you could stand on it to do the work.

Where would we get the money? "Take the cash and let the credit go," Omar said, "nor heed the rumble of a distant drum." We were young. I would get a raise and somehow we would find the means to borrow and pay. Then we would live happily ever after for two weeks in the summer.

We would not have a castle and a full-rigged ship to keep in a boathouse, nor even a cottage with servants, tea on the lawn, and a boatman in uniform to pilot a gleaming launch. We would have two used outboard motorboats and an unkempt property with a house with a broken dock and a broken roof—and something more than this. If anyone had asked why we needed this and what the something more might be, neither Margaret nor I could have answered at the time.

It was difficult to believe in summer when we crossed the Bridge to return to my job at the end of that three-day winter weekend. Ice was forming in the river, as Will said it would, and snow was falling so thickly that from the top of the Canadian arc we could not see either end of the span.

4

We returned to Maryland, where we lived apart together. We had been married for ten years and yet we had never had a home. Like most of our generation, we lived instead in a kind of programmed limbo. We had spent the first three years necessarily apart. Margaret lived in a one-room apartment in Philadelphia with a baby and I in tents pitched in various jungles of the Southwest Pacific Theater of Operations. Now we lived apart together in a little house in the Maryland countryside. Each day Margaret had her baby to tend, the dishes to wash, the beds to make, the chickens to feed, and the neighbors' Holsteins for company. The older children would climb each morning into a Halloween-painted omnibus to descend miles away at a shiny new school that looked exactly like a shiny new factory. There they learned to curl into fetal positions in corridors when the siren called them to practice against the promised moment when a light, brighter than any sun, would signal the end of the world. Each day I would rise at three so as to be in Washington at four, where I spent my powers describing crimes and disasters for the benefit of one hundred and forty thousand subscribers.

The house was pleasant enough and so were the surrounding low and folded hills. The lawn, the garden, and the henyard added to our pleasures, but this was a habitation not of our choice but of necessity. The alternative—to live closer to the city and so, in a sense, closer to much that was as important and as necessary to us as mind is to body—was to live in a little box built on a concrete slab. The house in the country was at least something, a kind of boarding house which the children and I visited as overnight guests and weekend lodgers. But we were no more a family than a seed, lying below the frost line, is a tree.

We lived a series of identical, unconnected days, the free citizens of the richest, most powerful nation on earth, unable to determine exactly what was missing. Our Maryland winter was not precisely one of discontent. It had its fogs and freezing rains, but the weather was not unbearable. There are worse winters elsewhere. Seen from the aspect of eternity, the job I had was silly, but I could do it well enough and rather liked doing it. Margaret was reasonably happy. No one, including Freud, has ever been able to say what it is that women

57

want, but she had no more particular complaints than I. As far as I could see, the older children had no problems they could not solve, and the youngest one had none at all so long as her demands were met. Just then all that she demanded was milk, sleep, love, and a dry diaper.

Yet, looking back on that fallow time, we apparently sensed that what we had was not enough. It was not that we envied others possessions; we were impervious to advertising. Nor did we envy the lives that other people led. We simply did what we could as well as we could do it within the terms that seemed to have been given us. We accepted living apart from each other for most of the day as a normal social condition; accepted the factory-school because there was no other; regarded the air-raid siren as part of the familiar furniture of our time; and looked forward to my advancement in my profession. And although we were not unhappy in our situation, we both felt that it would never do to live this way forever.

Our thoughts now, however, were elsewhere. They had to do with a world where the vital questions concerned the changing level of a river, the varying direction and speed of the wind, the relationship of hay and rainfall, breaking stone, the different uses of different kinds of wood, the thickness of the ice, raising children, comforting the sick, burying the dead. We thought of Rockport and we thought continually of our island.

The older children, nine and six, were curious and immediately excited. They had of course been to the river in summer, and they wondered which island it was and how big it was; they looked forward to being pirates. They were greatly interested in the boats. We told them that Uncle Bob had loaned us the old cypress sailboat that Will had converted into an outboard hull and that he had also loaned us the old five-horsepower Montgomery Ward engine to put on it till we could buy a boat and motor of our own. The other boat was the one we had bought from Chub. The children were delighted to hear that it had a ten-horsepower engine and went so fast it scared you. To a child, however, next week lies in a remote future, and next summer lies at some far end of time. Their excitement vanished almost as soon as it had been aroused. Only a vague curiosity remained, which surfaced now and again as Margaret and I continued to discuss our future needs.

Christmas must have been a disappointment for the children when they came whispering and tiptoeing downstairs in the predawn dark to turn the tree lights on, only to discover fishing leaders, lures, and swivels in their stockings, along with the candy canes. Christmas was more for the island than for them. There were screwdrivers, pliers, a brace and bits, a set of wrenches, an ax, saw, hammer and whetstone beneath the tree. One large, heavy and impressively wrapped package contained a coil of Manila line; another enclosed an anchor. There were war surplus parkas, blankets, and ponchos. Our Christmas shopping had taken one day, most of it spent at an Army-Navy store. The two baitboxes each contained a tin drinking cup for dipping over the side when we would be hot and thirsty on the river in the impossibly remote summer. Christopher, our nine-year-old, was reasonably pleased with his boy-sized casting rod, but what can a small boy do with a casting rod on Christmas

Day on a snowy lawn in Maryland? Fortunately, the grandparents had thought of electric trains and dolls, but there were grandparental gifts for the island, too. One was a rope ladder. Another was a hammock. One of my presents to Margaret was a secret. She would not know what it was till she saw it in the boathouse.

We kept talking about the island to our friends, although there was no way we could describe it, for we had no common points of reference. We said they must all come to visit, and they politely said they would. We said we had now joined the gay, carefree, international yachting set, what with having an island in Canada and two boats, but unfortunately we did not leave it there. Our friends were all Washington newspapermen and their wives, and the conversation on social occasions in this circle normally takes the form of shoptalk. Unlike other shoptalk, that of newspaper people is never narrow. Ranging over the whole world of ideas in action, it is customarily informed, shrewd, and, in a good sense of the word, clever. For us to have nattered on about our island was much as if we had described thrilling hands of Old Maid to a convention of bridge experts.

I suppose that our preoccupation with the island had to do with a concept of home. No one has ever defined the word to to my entire satisfaction, but I think that home embraces concepts of peace, security, and well-being. You find comfort in its familiar looks, sounds, and smells, and you also believe it to be beautiful. In the latter context, I suppose that none of us is really happy in any kind of country different from the one he first knew as a child. For example, I know a Colorado mining engineer who is never wholly content until he finds himself on a lonely mountainside. I know a woman from Kansas who cannot abide hills; she feels trapped without a big sky and far horizons. I know a great many more people who need the sound of traffic in city streets in order to be able to sleep at night and who need the constant company of civic multitudes in order to feel themselves a part of life. Even though they may never go to their city's theaters, concerts, museums, or galleries themselves, they need to know that they live where civilization exists.

Next, home must be a place where you enjoy living every day of your life; to which you gladly return whenever you have been away; where you face no threats, have no enemies, meet no strangers. Above all, it must be a place where you can relax, take your shoes off, and be yourself. We spend most of our days, Eliot said, preparing a face for the faces we must meet. But at home you should not have to do this. When people speak of bad homes, or broken ones, of running away from home, or hating to go home, they suggest the absence of most or all of these rather mysterious things. Finally, home is something you must help to create. I have never believed those real-estate advertisements that say "Homes for Sale."

All our talk about our Canadian island in the summer was not about an escape from life but rather about the possibility of an escape to it. After ten years of marriage we had at last acquired something that was not programmed, something of our choosing. By the rational standards of the programmed life we had been living, our purchase of the island made no sense whatsoever; indeed, our choice was more a spontaneous response than a carefully considered reasonable act. Yet it held forth the promise that, at least for two weeks in every year, we would find ourselves at home.

PART TWO

Spring

5

"First," Will said, sinking to his knees on the ruinous dock in the early-morning sunlight, "we'll have to study it out."

He knelt with his hands on his knees, the aquiline nose more prominent with his long, thin features impassive; the crows' feet and seams in the old cheeks were tribal marks; his eyes saw nothing as he stared across the still water.

Will knew, after studying things out, how to put in a dock that would stay where he put it, or how to design trusses that would carry the weight of a roof over to and down on the outside bearing walls. He never worked out the weights and stresses and parallelograms of forces with paper and pencil; he simply knew what they would be. If Will had had a university education the world would have been the richer for a great civil engineer. But since he lacked a high-school education, Rockport was the richer instead. Everyone in Rockport waited for Will to study things out before attempting complicated work. David Farrar and I stood silent, waiting for the words of the sachem.

"Now you might better take her all out," he said at last, looking at me, "and save all the good boards in her."

He drew a ten-penny nail from his coat pocket and made a diagram in the soft pine plank before him. He wanted us to do away with the long broken dock that, running parallel with the boathouse, formed an outside boat slip. We should instead build a new, triangular dock, using the still-sound stringers and boards of the old one. It could stretch from a point along the boat-house wall to the stone-filled crib at the land end of the dock on which he knelt.

"That way," he said, "you'll have a place where you can sit out. If I was you, I'd leave the cribs where they are. They'll help keep the ice away from the boathouse, and that first crib will give the kids something to swim to when they're learning to swim. You can deck the last one over and use her for a swimming dock—you can put a diving board on her.

"Now up here," he said, rising and looking into the clear water, "you might better put in a load of stone to make an ice break. When the ice starts to move, she'll

66

come right along here in the current, and if you put a couple of scow-loads of stone right here, the ice will hit the stone and go out that way, away from the boat-house."

He left to survey the broken stairs and to talk with Margaret about the coal-oil hot-water heater, while David and I labored with crowbars, mauls, and hammers, taking the dock apart as carefully as we could. We made a pile of good boards and another of spoiled ones that we would later cut and split for kindling. David had left his farm that day to help me, and in mid-morning my son came to join us. Of course there is no one in this world more willing to work, more anxious to assist, and more entirely inept than a nine-year-old boy. I put him to work taking old nails out of boards, not expecting him to do so for very long, and sure enough a matter of greater importance soon commanded his entire attention.

"Dad!" he said. "Look at that fish!"

I had a glimpse of a great, dark shadow disappearing into the shadows of the deep-water weeds.

"He was that long!" Christopher said.

"That there was pike," Will said.

He had silently rejoined us.

"Let me show you something," the old man told Chris. "If you was to put this block of wood right here, you can pry on it, and you won't have to pull so hard or bend that nail so much."

"How big do you think he was?" Chris asked.

"Oh, five pounds anyway. There, see how easy she came out? I remember a time," Will said, "when we were downriver once in the spring, putting in a dock for a fellow who had a farm, when we saw a big bass. Four and a half pounds he was."

"Did you catch him?"

"Not exactly," the old man said. "It was a day like this, with the water this still, so you could look right down to the bottom, just as clear as anything. We saw the bass because a fellow dropped a nail, and he looked to see it going down, and there come a bass, looking at that bright, new nail.

"We could see the nail on the bottom and the bass hanging there in the water, looking at it, when just like that a muskie came out from under the dock where we was and got him."

David and I stopped what we were doing.

"He came and took him and turned him the way they do and swallowed him right down head first while we was watching," Will said. "Then he started away, swimming slow near the top of the water, and the other fellows, they had to jump in the boat and go after him. They was going to cast for him. But I stayed where I was, because a muskie will always come back to where you've seen him feed. They hunt along a regular trail, muskies do, and sooner or later they'll be back again. So I went to the barn and got a pitchfork and went back to where we was working and just sat there and kept quiet and waited for him. After a while along he comes, and when the fellows got back with the boat after looking for him all over the river, I had that muskie for them."

"You speared it?" I asked.

"I could have speared him if I'd had a spear," Will

68

said. "But all I could do with that pitchfork was just put it to him as hard as I could and hold him down on the bottom till he stopped thrashing around. It was a way down, so I only had ahold of the handle near the top, leaning on it, and it was all I could do to hold him, the way he was thrashing, but after a while I had him.

"That," Will said, "is how I know what the bass weighed, because the bass was still fresh in his stomach when we cleaned him, so that night we not only had the muskie, we also had the bass."

It sounded like a fish story, but Will was a good fisherman, and good fishermen never tell stories about fish.

"That muskie went fifty-two pounds," Will said. "There was more than enough fish for everybody, so I kept the bass for myself."

"Will the pike come back?" Chris wanted to know. "Do we have a pitchfork?"

"When you get through with them nails, you might want to try casting for him," Will said.

We had Will's help in many things in the beginning —the help we requested in addition to that which he thought necessary. But some things we had to sort out for ourselves. One morning, feeling the wind rise, listening to the creaking ropes as the boats rode uneasily at their moorings below, seeing the rain driving in sheets across the gray river, setting out cooking pots to catch the drops leaking through the roof, and wondering when the weather would clear, we found ourselves confronted by certain less enchanting aspects of the insular life. The electrical system, always temperamental, had failed entirely that morning. Until Ed Huck could repair the power plant, we could not pump water. We would have to carry it in pails from the river. A more crucial matter was what we would eat that night, for apart from a can of peaches and a bag of popcorn, there was no food in the house. This was the day we were to have gone to the store.

The day wore on, growing darker rather than lighter. The rain rattled against the windowpanes, seeped in around the frames, and dribbled down the hall from beneath the front door. At four in the afternoon we were telling each other we should have gone to Rockport in the morning, because it was worse out now than it was then. We also told ourselves to wait a bit, because the wind would drop in the late afternoon. Instead, the wind kept rising. At length there was nothing else for it. Rain or not, a trip to shore was necessary.

We went across the river in the small, slow outboard motorboat, with the rain working in around our collars and running down inside our clothes, and spray, driven by the wind, bursting over the bows no matter how slowly we tried to take the waves. In the middle of the Canadian channel we found a heavy sea running. The northeast wind, working up against the current, piled up great hills of water. The wind was blowing the tops off these rollers, and we swam precariously up and down over the waterhills that were larger than our boat, pitching, yawing, and rolling about in a wet smother. Not only were we sopping inside our rain gear, but water was sloshing in the bilge—bailing with a tin can was an exercise more hopeful than efficient.

Ed Huck, the only man on the river who understood the mysteries of our electrical system, said he could come out to the island on Monday. We would carry water for the next three days, it seemed. There was plenty of water, at any rate—above, below, and all around us. We moved wetly off to Collins' store, whose only advertising display was a sign in the window. WORMS, it said.

By the time we had crept back to our island across two miles of windy downpour, the potatoes, the beets, and the bacon were soaking in ankle-deep water in the bilge. The sodden paper bag had turned to pulp. The bread, which Margaret carried beneath her raincoat, was not entirely damp.

"It's different," she said as we warmed ourselves luxuriantly before the hearth while our wet clothing steamed on the fire screen. "It's not like going to the supermarket."

"Next time," I said, "we must remember to bring a pail to put the groceries in and a poncho to cover the pail."

"What we really need," she said, "is a Northeaster Shelf in the pantry with a three-day supply of canned goods."

"And a bilge pump," I said. "We ought to carry a bilge pump. Bailing with a tin can is like nothing at all."

"What are we going to do about the lights?" she wanted to know.

"One of two things," I told her. "Either I take a

degree in electrical engineering, or we can figure out a way to do without that damned plant. What with Huck's repair bills and the price of gasoline, it costs about eighty cents an hour to generate electricity, and anyway there will not always be an Ed Huck around to help us."

The wind kept rising that night to near-gale force. We knew something about three-day northeasters. In prior summers, when we had visited at Bob's mainland cottage, a three-day blow simply meant that you did something other than swim and fish while waiting for the weather to break. You could, for example, drive to Kingston to see Old Fort Henry, or up to Ottawa to see the Parliament buildings and then have lunch at Henry Burger's restaurant in Hull. If you lived on the mainland and had an automobile, there were many places you could go in bad weather. But now we learned what it was to be marooned on a wet island for three days, and the older children discovered the possibilities afforded by the holes in the front-bedroom floor.

That bedroom had once been a kitchen; water pipes had passed through those holes. Christopher and his six-year-old sister Margaret looked down through them to see suspended in gray-green deep water shoals of rock bass, perch, and bluegills who had come, apparently, to share the storm with us. A line, a sinker, a hook, and a worm were instantly procured. Our house was, the children explained, the only one in the world where you could catch fish in the bedroom. Their delightful problem was that the fish were too large for the holes. When one brought a flopping bluegill up out of the water, the other would shriek the good news to us and go pounding down the hall and down the outside stairs and into the boat slips to receive a fish lowered carefully down from the ceiling. It was, as Margaret said, different. It was different from living on the mainland, where fun, almost by definition, means something that takes place away from home; different too from vacationing in someone else's house or a motel, where everything is done for you.

When the weather cleared we returned to the river and to the three pleasures that had been primarily responsible for our purchase of the island. The first of these was fishing, the original attraction of the St. Lawrence for the first vacationers. In the mornings Chris and I would cast from the dock and often enough have a good bass or pike cleaned, boned, cut into pieces, and ready to be shaken in a bag of seasoned flour by the time the coffee was done and the bacon crisp. After breakfast we would go out on the water to combine the pleasure of fishing with the other two principal pleasures—exploring and swimming. We would troll slowly downriver along the edges of weedbeds, turning the boat to drag the big Skinner spoons in and out of coves and beside deep-water rocks that seemed to promise large fish lying in the shadow. We could have taken more fish if we had anchored over a deep hole in the river floor and still-fished with live minnows, but we trolled because we loved to savor, slowly, the constantly changing shapes of stones and trees and water as the islands slid by. In those days, when many of the islands had no houses on them, we would put ashore on a deserted island to swim, build a fire, and cook the fish we had caught for lunch, then

troll slowly home in red sunsets that made black silhouettes of island pines.

Whenever we trolled thus, our persistent hope was
to land a fish such as Will described. You can see them
lying under skim ice in the shallows in the spring, hanging in clear water beneath a windowpane of ice, predators built for speed and armed with rows of long, sharp,
double-edged teeth, their fins gently moving. These are
what you hunt in summer: the enormous pike and their
even larger cousins the muskellunge. The record catch
on rod and reel was a muskellunge that weighed more
than sixty-nine pounds and was caught some thirteen
miles upriver from our island. When you see them in the
shallows in the spring they are spawning and you may
not fish for them then. At this time of year, however,
hungry men to whom need is more compelling than any
game law shoot or spear them as they lie.

These fish feed near shore at dawn and dusk, so lore
says, but we always hoped, and so we trolled baits astern
whenever we were on the water. One bright afternoon,
when Margaret and I were returning from Rockport with
bread and milk, trolling as we moved along the edge of
the cliffs below McGoogan's Point, the river exploded
ahead of us.

"Did you see that!" I shouted.

Of course, facing astern, she had not seen it.

But in the next moment she was fairly pulled from
her seat on the thwart, desperately hanging onto a rod
almost snatched from her hands.

"Bottom!" she said. "Back up. I'm on bottom! No,
it isn't! It's moving!"

74

The bottom of the river, if that is what she had, was moving rapidly and steadily out toward the channel away from the cliffs.

"I don't know if I can hold him," she said. "Oh, I've got a fish! I've got a fish!"

Just how long she would have it seemed an interesting question. The vision I had, when the river exploded, was of a vast dark shape at the center of the explosion. Margaret was fishing with her grandfather's old steel trolling rod. There was no star drag on this rod, just a leather thumb tab. You were supposed to apply pressure on this tab as the line came off the reel, enough pressure to slow the fish and hold him so that he would exhaust himself fighting the whip in the rod but not so much as to break the line. The line was made of black cotton and, when new, whenever that may have been, was supposed to support a weight of twelve pounds.

I had shut the motor off, but we, too, were moving out toward the channel and against the current. As the line began to slant up out of the water, Margaret raised the rod tip up and back, reeling as fast as she could, guiding the line in even loops with her left thumb. Angling consists of maintaining an angle formed by rod and line. When that huge, slab-sided fish came boiling out of the water, walking for a moment on his thrashing tail and shaking that great, toothed head, showing us those silver sides with the dark, circular blotches on them, Margaret succeeded in keeping that angle and the line taut.

And away he went down again, now speeding beneath the bows of the boat, with Margaret scrambling to keep the line from fouling beneath.

75

Again and again he jumped, shaking his great head, then flashed under the stern to send Margaret piling over me to keep the line from the motor. All this went on for more than half an hour before Margaret had him swimming slowly near the surface, drawing him ever closer to the boat.

Magnified by the water, that fish looked nearly as long as the oar. The next problem would be landing him. Some fishing guides carry .22-caliber Colt Woodsman pistols to shoot muskies at boatside. Most carry gaffs. The ones who carry pistols are those who do not want to run the risk of having their arms broken when a heavy muskellunge, thrashing beside the boat, breaks the gaff handle free from the guide's grasp and cracks his arm with it. One way to land a muskie is to work him into the shallows, go over the side yourself, and beach him. Guides recommend this. But no matter how you land a muskellunge, all the guides advocate hitting him over the head at once, and they all carry something heavy, such as a jemmey or a tire iron, for this purpose. You no more want a live muskellunge flopping around in your boat than you would want a live barracuda. There are all those grinning teeth, and, apart from them, there is a great deal of power in that smashing tail.

With the fish coming toward us, rolling now on the water with his air bladder full and his power momentarily spent, I began to consider the problem. I had no pistol, no gaff, no net (and there was no hand net that would ever hold this fish), and no crowbar. All we had in the boat was a loaf of bread and a quart of milk. Nor was there any beach; we were on a cliff shore.

"Easy," I told her. "Just bring him along easy. You're doing fine. Here he comes."

I pulled gently on the line while Margaret as carefully reeled. I wanted to get hold of the copper-wire leader. With the leader in one hand, I would close my other hand over the top of his head, crushing in on the gill plates, and, with both hands at once, swing him in over the gunwales. Then I'd hit him with an oar.

"Oh, he's huge," Margaret said.

He was a great, dark-backed, orange-finned, silver-flanked muskellunge, the largest fish I had ever seen at boatside. He was larger than our son. His head was as big as a football.

"Just keep him coming like that," I told her. I could feel Margaret trembling; her reeling was just the least bit jittery.

"The leader is all the way down his throat," I told her. "All right, now I've got him!"

Since I could not grasp the copper leader, I held the line while I grabbed the fish over the back of the head, squeezed, and with both hands lifted him out of the water.

That heavy tail smashed against the gunwale with a force that shook the boat. My hand skidded on the slippery wet gill plates, and as the head slipped through my fingers the weight of the fish broke the line. I grabbed for him again as he lay for an instant beside the boat in the water.

Margaret sat on the thwart and cried.

Somebody once told us that the fish that gets away is the best one of all, because he keeps getting bigger each time you tell the story. I disagree. The muskellunge that Margaret caught that day, fought for more than half an hour, played beautifully, and brought perfectly to the side of the boat never got away. Instead, I lost it. Nothing will ever make up for that, and I will always see that wonderful fish, a trophy fish if ever there was one, lying in the water for the instant it took to recover before it slowly and then more rapidly sank swimming down out of sight in deep water.

One day that spring in the spring of our lives we went exploring upriver with Will and Effie. It was one of those crystal northwind days when the farther islands stand above the horizon between sky and water, when objects in the distant background seem more sharply etched than those in the immediate foreground. There was just a riffle on the water, enough of a northern zephyr to keep us cool in the bright sunshine, and we followed the Canadian channel upriver and into the maze beneath the bridge. Will showed us the whirlpools and the shoals. There was a great expanse of open river above the maze, but in the distance we could see the red and black buoys that marked the channel. Beyond them on the horizon was another group of islands: Dumbfounder, Belaborer, Deathdealer, and Bloodletter, they were called, but past them you came to Camelot if all went well.

Our destination was Grindstone Island, some fifteen miles from our own. Will wanted to show us the safe route up and around the head of Grindstone and down this time in the American channel, along the American flanks of Wellesley Island, past Alexandria Bay, and so across the river to our island again. It was as important for us to learn the river as it is for a city child to learn his way from home to school. You cannot always simply follow the buoys, because the unlighted ones are invisible at night and because the river is not buoyed save in the ship channels. Nor can you always follow the charts with absolute faith. Not every rock and shoal is charted. On this day we were shoal-hunting as well as learning some thirty-five miles of water paths that were new to us. "Now go over a bit that way, JK. Go slow. She ought to be almost anywhere right here," Will would say, and we would come drifting up, with the motor off, to suddenly shallowing water, and hastily put out an oar to fend off the yellow boulders appearing beneath the bow.

"Now you see you'd never know them rocks was there," Will would say. "It looks like good water all across here. But when you put your bow on that barn and when you have that island right straight abeam, you'll hit her every time."

We looked for shoals not only in order to avoid them but also because, Will said, "Now there's dandy fishing right off the head of this one," or, "When there's too much west wind other places, you can always try about ten yards off the other side of where we are now."

Will taught us to look for changing color on the water surface; to watch for waves that had no apparent reason to appear where they did; to remember that you could not always count on deep water near a cliff shore, or shallow water off shelving rock. The latter was a general rule with many exceptions.

Grindstone is a large island with many farms. At noon in a sheltered cove, we moored to a large, decaying dock of gray beams and treacherous planks. There were yards of water beneath the dock. Great sailing ships once moored here to take on granite from the quarry behind it. The quarry was as deserted as the crumbling pier. The streets of Chicago were paved with stone from that quarry, Will said, and the pillars of the State House at Albany came from there. But that was in the time before, as the local people said, the price fell out of the stone, and I wondered if the modern use of cement had something to do with it. But I particularly wondered how large sailing vessels had come upriver the way we had, against the current with the prevailing wind dead foul, and no room to reach or tack. They used to kedge them up, Will said, remembering those days. Ships' boats would take lines ashore and make them fast to the boles of trees, and the crew about the capstans, or steam winches, would haul the vessels ahead. When the cable was made up, the ship would anchor in the current while the cable was payed out again to a farther tree. Apparently the price fell out of the stone before steamships used the river, although I could not be sure of the chronology. In any case, Will remembered the sailing ships. He had lived on Grindstone as a boy and learned, at the quarry, where to strike with a maul to break the rock most easily.

A path led inland from the quarry through a forest where, in a dingle, there were hare bells and trillium, and, in magnificent isolation, the largest birch tree we had ever seen. It was several feet in diameter and tall as a great white pine. "You don't see trees like that much anymore," Will somewhat unecessarily said, "but that there is a canoe birch." It was from such great trees, and not from the slender, decorative little birches, that the Indians and early settlers made their birchbark canoes. So Will said, and looking at this huge tree, we could understand why. Carefully peeled, the bole would have provided a single sheet of bark long and wide enough to have formed a thirty-foot canoe. Will did not believe the small birches, with which we were familiar, grew into canoe birches. He thought they were different trees. There were white birches, yellow birches, and canoe birches, he said. We supposed, although we had no way of knowing, that the reason we had never seen a canoe birch before was that all the others had been made into canoes more than a hundred years ago, or that this was the survivor of some disease that had killed the others. Will did not know either, but he was inclined to doubt the first theory because, he said (perhaps drawing upon the memory of an Indian ancestor), "They made canoes mostly out of elm, not birchbark. Elm was stronger. There was a lot of elm back then, so they wouldn't have to use the birch. But that there is a canoe birch, just the same."

The bit of forest verged on pastureland, and we followed a dirt road to the village of Thurso, where there was a church and a school. The entire population was having games and a picnic in the schoolyard. Will immediately left us to embrace an elderly woman who, first astonished and then delighted, returned his kisses.

"My," Effie said. "There he goes again. Will was always a great one for kissing the girls."

She was not at all pleased that the woman had been one of Will's girls when he had been a boy on Grindstone Island.

While Will and Effie visited with people they had not seen in years, for reasons that may have had to do with the Grindstone Island farmers keeping much to their island and themselves, Margaret and I were fascinated by the children, especially intrigued by their dress. They looked like an illustration from Kate Greenaway's books, complete to the girls' poke bonnets and high-buttoned shoes and the roundabouts of the boys. This was not, however, a costume picnic but a simple, rural festival, with everyone dressed in his best. It was a community that tended its fields, kept a school, went to church, and took its own deep pleasure in a picnic in the schoolyard where men and boys played baseball, pitched horseshoes, and flirted with girls in poke bonnets, and the little children played Red Rover. The village simply kept a different time from Eastern Standard or Daylight Saving.

So, too, did the cheese factory. We found it on a country road, a long, low building with a row of metal milk cans beside its door. Inside we found the cheese-maker, a man the complexion of his cheddar who spent each day from five in the morning to ten at night with his rennet, curds, whey, wooden paddles, and cheese press. The farmers brought him milk, which he would make into cheese. The factory operated on the principle of a cooperative. The forming cheese was shaped by a hand-screw press into ninety-pound wheels, which, bound in cheesecloth, were then set to age in a dim, cool stone room. The war was a great disaster for the cheesemaker because, he said, the Army "took all I could make as fast as I could make it, and you want to let it age at least a year. It used to make me sick to think of fellows having to eat that new cheese." His only other disappointment in life was that his wife did not like cheese. Now, he loved it, he said, cutting us wedges from an aged wheel and carving wedges for himself, "and I always have a bit every time I get a chance. But," he said, "I can't get her to have any at all. I keep saying she don't know what she's missing, but she keeps saying no."

We added a pound of what on one side of the river is called New York Sharp and on the other Canadian Cheddar to the picnic we had with Will and Effie, sitting in the shade of young oaks on the once valuable granite of Grindstone Island, looking across the blue river.

"All out there," Will said, pointing with his chin, "where you see those boats, is Forty Acre Shoal. In the fall you'll see ten, twenty boats out there. There'll be fellows in them all the way from Texas, trolling for muskies."

"If we ever came up for a weekend in the fall, would you take us out?" I asked.

"Well, yes, I think I would," Will said. "Oh, you can catch a dandy in the fall."

A weekend in fall was not what I wanted. I wished, on that spring day, that we could stay on the river and let fall come to us.

6

At noon on Friday I would leave behind the steaming tropical heat and melting asphalt of Washington and drive through air that, until I was on the mountain that looks down on Syracuse, had all the piquant freshness of the exhaust fan of a Turkish bath. It would then be nine o'clock at night, with still a good bit of light in the west; but by the time I escaped the dull squalor of Syracuse three quarters of an hour later, it would be dark, and there would still be another three hours to go before I reached the river. Bone-weary, stiff-legged, and generally groggy from a twelve-hour experience of negotiating narrow roads at speed, I would crawl out of the car and climb into the boat. But the instant the boat moved out into the dark river, fatigue gave way to alert pleasure. Perhaps stepping from car to boat involved a change of mental gears that, in turn, moved physical ones. In any case, the metamorphosis was instantaneous.

It was wonderful to be alone on the river at midnight. I soon discovered that a star culminated precisely over our island and that once I had cleared Noble's Point, which forms a shoulder of the Bodines' cove, I could steer on that star without reference to the dark shapes of the islands. There were no shore lights. There were only the running lights on the outboard and those of the stars swinging through sidereal time. The only sounds were the plashing of the bow wave and the burble of the engine astern. Margaret would wait up for me, and when she saw the little red and green lights bobbing toward her through the night, she would prepare melted cheese sandwiches with Canadian bacon and set out a cold bottle of ale. That was wonderful, too.

Not so wonderful was having to leave the island at four on Sunday afternoon in order to arrive back in Washington at four on Monday morning. The unwonderful aspects were not confined to the routine horrors of happy motoring. They involved rather the reverse changing of those mental gears. This time the change was from life to job. While I could not have asked for more congenial colleagues or a happier newspaper than the *Washington Daily News*, I began to question the nature of work itself. It seemed to me, as that first island summer passed, that the word *job* derived exactly from the name of the man who had the first one.

As interesting as my job was, it could be considered

from a canine point of view. Five days a week, for fifty weeks each year, I would fetch thrown sticks, jump over hurdles, bark, sit up and beg, roll over and play dead. In return, I would receive a pat on the head, my Kennel Ration, and a place to sleep. Every weekend my master would slip my leash so that I could run around the lawn, and for two weeks out of the fifty-two he made no demands on me. I had the kindliest of masters, whom I genuinely loved, and I gladly licked his hand. Good dog, he said, and gave me an extra bone.

Anyone who takes this canine point of view may discover a difference between working like a dog for a living and being kept as a pet with a job. A job is something you do because someone else has hired you to do it for him. Work, however, you do because you need and want to do it; to work is to create out of your imagination that which is valuable to others but which never before existed. A carpenter takes wood, tools, brushes, and a can of stain and out of these elements creates something different from any of them: a chair. If he labors in a furniture factory, making parts of chairs to someone else's pattern for a third man to glue together for a fourth to stain for a fifth to sell to a middleman who consigns them to a retailer who deals with a total stranger, then that carpenter has a job. But if he labors for himself in his own house, adding his vision to his tools and materials, creating chairs to his own invented patterns, and offers them to people who are pleased with his labors and who want to take them to their homes to become a part of their lives, then that carpenter is at work.

86

Spring

I had an intimation of this difference twenty years ago, while yo-yoing up and down the highways between Washington and Canada in a glass-and-metal capsule. In those days a great many national magazines bought articles from writers. It occurred to me that I could write as well as some whose bylines headed the articles. I put this observation to the test. An article I wrote in a few after-job hours was purchased for the same amount of money I earned in a week on my job. Why not work for myself? The prospect was as tantalizing to me as a field to a hunting dog that, heretofore confined to a city apartment, now has a vision of what life ought to be. But that vision might never have come to me if we had not bought the island and if the island had not exerted a possibly mysterious but certainly insidious influence on us.

The island was becoming more and more a place to live and less and less a place to spend a summer vacation. My secret Christmas present to Margaret had been to commission Will's son, Edson, to repaint the living room. What had been a dark-brown room with brown pictures in darker frames was now sunny and cheerful at first light, with reflected ripples dancing on the white ceiling and sunlight glowing on the yellow walls. Men put windows in houses, and women put curtains in the windows. I have never understood what makes women want to do this, but I must agree that Margaret's choice was impeccable, restrained, and altogether lovely. In what we still call the five-and-ten, she found valences and tie-back curtains with a pattern in green, beige, white, and black. The pattern was of birch trees, and these curtains not only complemented the yellow walls and white ceiling and tended to make the great room appear comfortably smaller, but they also were entirely appropriate and complementary to the island itself. The view from the windows was one of blue water, and now you saw this as if from within a grove of birches. There were green grass rugs on what had been bare boards and new crimson cloth on the pillows that formed the upholstery of the once brown sofa and easy chairs. The crimson echoed that of the fireplace and chimney bricks, and on either side of the chimney were shelves now filled with the varied colors of paperback books. Two wooden-and-wicker porch rockers had been given us, and Margaret covered their seats and backs with kapok-filled pads contained in a dull orange sailcloth. Black fire tools stood by the hearthstone and, next to them, the bright brass Cape Cod lighter. The pine table that had been on the dining porch was painted bright yellow and brought into the living room and placed beneath the west windows. The flag that had covered my uncle's coffin served as a cover for one of the brown flip-top tables, and its colors were reflected in the silvery bowl of the Aladdin lamp placed upon it. To those who said this might be a violation of flag rules, I could only say that it was my flag as surely as it was anyone's. There was also a home-made Jolly Roger on the wall, and the colors of the flags and all the colors of the room went somehow marvelously together. No matter what the weather or time of day, it was a wonderful room to be in. At night, with a fire on the hearth and a glow of red in what Margaret called the hotbellied stove, and with soft pools of light from the Aladdin lamps, we would play cards or chess with the children, or listen to Caruso or Paul Whiteman on the Victor Talking Machine. Our amusements were as eclectic as the room and, to us, as comfortable.

Color came to the porches, too. New dock gray went down on the floor of the cantilevered front porch, turned a corner, and went down the dining porch. The interior walls of the porches were white; the window frames, shutter-green. Margaret considered the ruinous chaise longue that had come with the house. Borrowing a book from the Alexandria Bay Library, she taught herself how to tie upholsterer's knots, bought waxed twine, tied the springs together again, and covered her newly upholstered chair with waterproof red boat-cushion plastic. She covered the cushions of the squeaky porch gliders with brightly striped awning cloth. A low wooden table painted a kind of pink, two small end tables of wrought iron and tile, and a little red rocking chair completed the furnishing of this porch—and all the various colors went as well together here as they had in the living room. We are now convinced that you cannot have too many colors in your house.

The bathroom and kitchen were repainted in pale green and white. The old zinc-lined wooden refrigerator chest had its top sanded smooth to serve as a bread board, and its sides became Chinese red trimmed in black. Margaret wanted a dragon painted on the white enamel bottle-gas refrigerator but has as yet to find the proper style and size in dragons. The children helped in all the painting, even six-year-old Victoria. We could not trust her with oil paints, but she did want to join in what we all were doing. Margaret told her she could use her watercolors to paint whatever she wished on the kitchen-cabinet doors. Victoria decorated them with a picture of a house and a border of flowers.

Essential repairs were in progress, and we dismantled that outhouse on the catwalk in order that our breakfast view did not include an old latrine. But it was not the physical changes alone that made the island seem increasingly homelike. Something else was astir, something that had to do with size, speed, time, and a sense of priority. The island was growing larger. More and more it was proving to be an enormous world in which we could largely live. At the same time, the outside world was shrinking. It was growing smaller and smaller, cramped because of its clutter.

In the city we were called upon to be attentive to and responsible for everything. We were supposed to be interested, and to some extent involved, in changing fashions, aid to India, professional football, tax schedules, the meaning behind what politicians said, the city's poor, dance styles, wayward youth, aircraft disasters, the lies of advertisers, whither the nation, nuclear war, the yelp and whine of the newest, most sensational pop singers, the book of the month that would be justifiably forgotten next month, the carpool, the lives of actresses, who said what to whom at cocktail parties, the price of eggs, and the imaginary differences in motorcars. All this, and a great deal more, was supposed to command our full attention all the time, and everything was made to appear just as crucially important as everything else. If we ignored something as stupid and silly, such as the Kentucky Derby, we were liable to be accused of being out of it—meaning out of touch with life. This city world lacked time in which to discover what was important, much less to live. Meanwhile, it was consumed by fear.

There was not then the fear of casual violence at any street corner but the fear of nuclear war. Houses in Virginia were advertised for sale as "outside the disaster area." There was fear that Moscow's agents, always depicted as enormously more clever than anyone else, were hidden in every government department. President Truman's witch hunt was on, preparing a climate in which such a weed as Senator Joseph McCarthy could flourish. More pervasive, and much more dangerous, was the fear of change. These were the days when David Riesman's "other-directed man" was anxiously looking around him to see what other people were doing in order that he could do it himself and thus be inconspicuous. All problems were represented as at a critical stage. *Crisis!* the newspapers shouted, not because *crisis* was a conveniently short headline word but because every day, if not every hour, there was an apparent crisis. Washington was not without its aspects of panic in a sheepfold.

By contrast, the island was a haven and a tower of vantage. All the world's problems were real enough, and all of them needed someone's attention, but neither were they all equally important, nor was anyone competent to deal at once with all of them. Everyone can, however, address his best efforts, in the areas of his competence, to matters that concern himself and others. This requires that you arrange these matters in the order of their importance within the framework of your competence to deal with them. This is difficult to do in the frenetic city where everyone shouts *crisis!* about the Community Chest one minute, the school curriculum the next, and demands that you care about the Pennsylvania miners and fluoridation of the local water at the same time you consider the prospects for war and peace. The island offered no isolation from the world but rather a place and time of relative calm in which to decide which dragons you could sally forth to slay. Everyone needs an island in his life where he can go to sort things out, even it is only an island he creates for himself in time, a sort of pit stop on the shoulder of the roaring rat race.

These thoughts became oppressive when the summer ended and we returned to Maryland. The little cottage at the head of the island with the seven views from the seven windows would make an office. I could go into the world, select a matter of interest to me and to others, learn enough to describe it, return to the island to write about it, and offer my view to the editors of the magazines. Of course there would be a certain element of risk. You have no way of knowing when, if ever, anyone might buy what you have spent a month writing; your income would be sporadic at best; you will have no medical benefits, vacations with pay, or pension plans provided by your employer; and, worse, you are the employer. As a livelihood, the career of a freelance writer may be compared with that of a hopeful prospector alone in the desert with his mule and his pans. There seemed to be, however, a unique form of workman's compensation: freedom. To this prospect the island offered the dimension of beauty set among the deep silences of the moving sky and moving water.

There came a day when I did not drive to Washington.

"Aren't you going to work today?" Margaret asked.

"Yes," I said, "I am. I've quit my job."

7

Everyone fishes for them. They are so thick in the water that baits are unnecessary. You throw out a hand-line festooned with treble hooks and snag several at a time. When they are swarming in their seething shoals, roiling the silt of marshes where feeder streams enter the river, bonfires are built on shelving rocks by the shore. The children caper around the fires like Indians, while women cook coffee, gossip, and heat bacon fat in skillets as the men and boys in rowboats and punts pull in fish by the hundred. You can see a fish fry from far across the night water: the flames on shore, the lights in the boats. You can hear it, and smell it too, before you come close enough to see light glinting from the wriggling fish being taken from the shallows.

Bullhead is the local name, though there may be a dozen names for the succulent little catfish that spawn in myriads in the spring.

There is a trick to cleaning them. Holding them carefully by the head, avoiding the barbels and the rather poisonous spines, you skin them with pliers. Competitions are held to see who can skin the most bullheads in the least time. You want to catch more than you think you will need because they are so good they will all be eaten. You can easily eat half a dozen of them yourself as you sit warming by the bonfire, taking fish hot from the skillet, drinking ale, and talking in the cold night with friends.

Bullheads are seldom seen during the rest of the year. Their arrival and the long-looked-forward-to fish fry is one of the rites of spring. There are other rites, too, including driving spiles into the maples when the sap begins to rise and having a boiling-off party to make maple syrup and sugar. There is a progression of portents and rites as spring comes tentatively to the river.

The first is a thaw that comes to spend a day or so in the very depth of the Canadian winter. It is like the church bell heard in the night, waking you to passing time but summoning no one to communion. Hearing the bell toll twice, you comfortably return to sleep. The next thaw, however, is like the bell that marks the half hour; you wonder which hour is half gone and stay uneasily awake until you hear the bell toll five o'clock. Now you move restlessly between reality and dreams, wishing you could remain in one state or the other while the river ice creaks and groans in an agony that can be heard miles away.

The heave, as the people call it, the sound that marks the passage of the winter night, comes when the river begins to rise. The river freezes solidly in midwinter while the water level is dropping. When the river is finally frozen, the shore ice is higher than that in midchannel, where the ice is floating on water. When the river begins to rise at winter's end, the depressed center of the ice rises with the rising water and enormous stresses are created as the concave surface tries to straighten. Where the riverbanks are marshes, the ice simply pushes inshore. But where the river squeezes between stone banks, something must give, and the cliffs will not. The ice is at least two feet thick; the pressure exerted by the rising water is enormous; the river groans. From upriver comes a sound like thunder but which, unlike thunder, does not roll away from you. Then you want to run to the riverbank to watch. As if a giant were ripping the river in two, the ice on one side of the channel rises abruptly, thrusts over the other, and sends ice blocks weighing several hundred pounds bursting into the air to fall with splintering crashes. The sound comes speeding toward you, growing louder and louder in a horrifying racketing now like that of an attacking aeroplane strafing toward you at ground level. And just when the noise becomes absolutely unendurable, it flies away downriver.

Thereafter, surface water slowly leaches the still-thick river ice, until at last a narrow channel appears in mid-river, growing slowly wider each day. The first ducks appear in dense flocks, splashing down to mate in ice water; willow stems turn yellow; the birches stir. There is still snow beneath the trees but not in pastures or on the rocks of the riverbank. The pike and muskellunge move toward the shallows, and you can hear geese calling to one another above the sullen clouds.

The return of the first water birds tells you that spring cannot be far away, but winter still envelops the world like the dark of that restless time before dawn when there is not yet the faintest light in the east. Thick wet snows may yet come, or, if not, days of sodden northeast gales and nights of frost. This is the longest, most wretched and exasperating time of all. One day there will be bright, hot sunlight and you can work in shirt sleeves and think spring has arrived at last—and then there will be a week of snow. Spring arrives teasingly, as if uncertain whether to come at all.

In Maryland there is first the snowdrop, then the crocus and hyacinth; later, the tulip and the rose. But in the Thousand Islands spring brings saxefrage, hepatica, trillium, and violets together with hare bells, ferns, and the blossoms of the fruit trees—followed at a little distance by wild roses, columbines, pinks, and all else that blooms in gardens, pastures, and forests. The now steadily warming days are filled with crystal light, and it is actually hot in sunny lees. Baby snapping turtles the size of dimes sun themselves on stones, huge carp smash about the roots of cat-o'-nine-tails, the bass drift over their spawning nests, and the spiders creep awake. In the red glow of spring evenings, what seems to be a thick, black, oily smoke eddies above the tops of the sun-warmed pines, and there is a sound like the hum of a giant dynamo. It is not smoke, however, but the mating flight of myriads of mosquitoes; the sound is the beating of their nuptial wings.

Simultaneous with the vast hatch of insects is the arrival of all the birds. The chickadees who have wintered over, and who can hang upside down in the air to take insects from the undersides of the new birch leaves, compete with the barn swallows, finches, and Baltimore orioles for their breakfasts. While geese and ducks are still coming through, flickers are drumming on the pines, great blue herons are standing sentinel along the shore-line, the solitary sandpipers teeter on the river stones. All the birds return in spring itself except the herring gulls, who await midsummer before coming to sit on the river shoals.

In the spring of our lives we would arrive on the river in late April before the spiders emerged from their winter corners. The river weather would still be uncertain, but we could wait no longer. When the dogwood blossoms lay in white levels through the Maryland forests and the peepers called at night, it was time for us to go. So on an April day, while the children were in school, we would assemble the going-to-Canada pile, which consisted of all the clothing and blankets we would need on the river and more that we never needed but took along anyway, together with the tools we carried back and forth. No matter now often we took the trip, we always carried too much. When the old Chevrolet taxicab gave way to a used station wagon, the station wagon was as overcrowded as the taxi had been. After supper we would load the children into the loaded car, making a nest of pillows on the floor for the baby and a bed for the older ones on the back seat, and drive through the night to Canada. The children offered no objections to their leaving school more than a month before the state of Maryland thought they should.

In the fresh, cold gray morning we would be on the roads that led through New York farms to the river, and everyone would watch for the first view, across the fields, of the high gray-green towers of the American span of the Thousand Islands Bridge. We all knew the first view of the towers came after you passed a barn between Lafargeville and Fishers Landing, but the first one to see them would win an ice-cream cone—provided, of course, that he remembered having won, because in the gathering excitement of going through customs, running down to the water to see if anyone had left our outboard motorboat at the mainland dock, packing the first load from the car into the boat, and moving out onto the stingingly cold water, he might forget.

There it is, we would all say at once, when, having cleared the foot of Club Island, we could see our island farther down the river. We always wondered whether it would still be there—not the island, of course, but the boathouse—as though this house that had come as if by magic into our lives might as suddenly vanish. A more substantial reason for our uncertainty was the possibility that the house had been damaged by ice or storms in the winter, or even burned down by the carelessness of the duck hunters or the thieves who regularly visited at some time between the day we left and the day we returned. As the island came closer, we would look carefully for damage to house and trees and see missing shingles, a broken shutter.

There was always a great deal to do, and there would have been more if we had waited for the insects to precede us, for then there would be spider webs everywhere, black and greasy with gnats. There was always winter dirt and dust, detritus from the trees, blown into the house. In the cold of the early morning we would search the house to see what might have been taken. Some young people in the area would, when planning marriage, help themselves to sheets, blankets, kitchenware, and tools. In addition to these homemakers, there was also the regularly jailed local kleptomaniac who, fortunately for the despoiled, kept everything he stole in neat good order in his house for the police to find and return. Rather than a menace, he could have been regarded as a faithful watchman if the law had taken another point of view. On our first return to the island, we missed a Coleman lantern, a pair of hip boots, a bucksaw, whetstone, ax, and Stilson wrench. Thereafter, we left no tools or anything else of much value on the island but carried them back and forth. Still, each year we would find some evidence of visitors.

While Margaret and I made a somewhat somber check on our chattels, the children more delightedly searched out well-remembered treasures of their own—Chris finding his book of knots and splices, Margaret her dolls, and Victoria emerging from the toy room, her arms full of stuffed animals. These surveys having been made, we would feel the fatigue of the long drive begin to return as we contemplated the chores of washing and mopping down the windows, walls, and floors of eight rooms in the boathouse—never mind yet the two stories of the bunkhouse and the cottage at the head of the island, nor the grass to whip down on the path, nor the other outboard that was still on blocks in the slip and had to be caulked and painted. But these could wait; first we would go out onto the porch that was cantilevered over the water and look down the passages of the great river and know why we had come. We were home and felt as if we had never been away. The immense view of sky and water and forested islands was as welcome and as necessary to us as the feel of earth beneath him was to Antaeus.

From the first time we stepped out there, we beheld our Promised Land, and every spring since we have gone to the porch before doing anything else. We are drawn there for reasons lying beneath pleasure. We enter subconsiously into a ritual of invocation, in sympathetic response to the rituals of spring taking place all around us. To do certain things exactly the same way each time you do them, and to do these things only at the same certain times each year, can be a way of entering into communion. We all sense in the return of birds in spring, and in the courses of the stars, the promise of a higher order, of a life continuing forever in the endless deeps of space and time. We accept or create mysteries or rituals in response to the natural rhythms of earth and heaven in order to feel ourselves at one with them. No matter what the ritual, and it may be a simple thing like going first to the porch before doing anything else, all our rituals are ways of touching base—and the base we all touch is that of God.

Within life's general timeless aspects there is of course constant change. The ancients discovered there was a time to live, a time to die, a time to destroy, a time to create. They also perceived these times were cyclical; to celebrate the mystery of eternally recurrent change within that which never changed, the Romans devised their lustral rites. Perhaps they noticed that human lives seem to divide neatly into five-year periods, that the child from one to five is quite a different child between five and ten—and so on through his life. For whatever reasons they hit upon it, the Romans thought in terms of lustrums. Each five years the people and city of Rome were purified and rededicated; it was a way of marking passing time in a world without beginning or end.

We, too, seem to have lived in lustrums on the island —a matter easily discernable now, although not in the beginning. We were, however, soon aware of the need to discover and closely follow the rituals appropriate to life on the river, of the need to read correctly the riddles of omens and portents. There was, for example, a need to live in harmony with the weather. After our first experience with that three-day northeaster that found us unprepared, we paid close attention to the sky. This might not be a matter of moment to city people, but when you live on an island you must come upon some way of making a daily forecast; your life itself may depend upon it, and your comfort most certainly will.

We learned the general truths that a mackerel sky is twelve hours dry; that mares' tails give you a day's grace; that a falling barometer means good fishing first and wind soon after; that a rising barometer means poor fishing but good weather on the way; that dew on the boats at night promises a clear sky tomorrow. We learned, too, that when all the birds apparently go mad, skittering about in the air neither for food nor for pleasure, it is a sure sign of something extraordinarily bad in the way of weather to come. The lonely call of the loon, not its inane laugh, is a portent of stifling heat. We looked to the southwest for our immediate forecasts, for the prevailing surface winds blow from that quarter, but not without also looking to see what difference there might be between the direction of the surface winds and that of clouds moving in the upper air. A simple book on meteorology taught us the names of the clouds, how to distinguish between warm and cold fronts from the shapes of the clouds, and what progression of weather to expect from each kind of frontal system as it moved over our island. We saw how the leaves turned backward and how the surface wind blows into an advancing thunderstorm, and we learned to judge from the weight of the wind how much time we had before the storm would strike.

Each morning Christopher would tap the barometer, check the temperature, go down to the dock to take the river's temperature, and enter these readings in a log we kept. When the river is at one temperature and the air at another, fog can suddenly close so thickly around you that you cannot see ten yards ahead. If you are on the river when it happens, you are in danger of holing the boat on a shoal or of being struck by another craft, and you will be a prisoner till the fog clears. Whenever there is a wind, there will also be a sea running. The wind can work for more than seven uninterrupted miles on many river reaches, and when the wind works on that much water, particularly if it blows against the current, there are going to be waves that will certainly drench you as you sit in an open boat—if they do not do more than that. When the wind will blow, and from whence, are important things to determine before setting out. Knowing them, you can then plot a course to take advantage of lees behind islands as you cross a stormy river. We looked to the spiders for long-range forecasts. The more spiders there are, and the sooner they appear in the spring, the greater the chance of a long, warm summer. At summer's end we paid close attention to the birds, for the sooner they leave the river, the longer and nastier the winter to come. One day in early September we saw the birds whirling crazily around the island and could think of no reason why they should. The cloudless day was bright and hot; it was, according to our log, ninety degrees Fahrenheit when we went swimming that afternoon, but half an hour after we were out of the water, drying and toasting on the dock, we could hear a wooshing sound in the north, like a giant blowing out the candles on his birthday cake, and the next minute we were flying indoors to close the windows against a heavy wind that on a fair and cloudless day dropped the temperature forty degrees at once. Next day the birds were gone. Snow came early that year.

If a certain amount of ritual was involved in trying to guess the mind of the weather gods, a quality of ritual was present in nearly all else that we did.

There is of course a great deal of ritual attendant upon fishing. Because fish are so easy to catch, you must create mysteries and complications for yourself in order to enjoy it. You can follow in the steps of the fisherman who will fish only with dry flies with a barbless hook on a horsehair line, carefully watching the wind, matching his flies to the insect hatch, casting only for brook trout. That fisherman is in his way summoning Fortuna and Neptune to his aid by means of intricate rituals, when if he simply wanted all the brook trout he could eat he could follow any country boy's example and still-fish with worms. The mysteries we made for ourselves involved never carrying a net when we were after pike or bass, trolling only with Skinner spoons along the weedbeds in certain water, doing everything in the same way each time. In this way we retraced our steps along well-loved water paths, always hopeful and expectant, never certain. There are many ways we could have been certain, but none of them was mysterious. Churchill once said, in effect, that without a vast uncertainty, life would lack a quality of adventure.

Each day we followed an unvarying pattern: work or chores in the morning, play when work was done. In this sense, they were like everyone else's days but with this important difference: The days were our own to fill, and we were never pressed for time. It was different from summers past when we had but two weeks on the river. Then, we seemed to need to be on the river every moment we could, busily vacationing all the time, with great emphasis on entertaining or being entertained. But now that we lived on the island the greater part of the year, our time expanded, leaving us free to wallow in the luxury of choice. It was the guests who smashed around the dock. They would arrive so tense from the city that they would flop around for the first three days before calming down enough to begin to see the islands. Then, unfortunately, they would have to leave. While we lived each day slowly, our guests jittered, and being hag-ridden by time, they could not understand that time can be whatever you wish to think it is. One day when Margaret said supper would be at six, because it would take an hour to prepare, a guest pointed out it was then a quarter to—whereupon Margaret simply reset the clock to show a quarter to five. This, she said, now gave her fifteen more minutes in which to visit on the porch before she had to start supper —which would then be ready at six.

"But you can't do that!" the guest protested. "You can't just change the clock!"

"I can if I want to," Margaret explained.

Larger time was not always accurate, either. There might be an early spring, or a late one. One year spring came late to Maryland and even later to Canada, as Christopher's entries in the log attest.

"May 24," he wrote. "Left Maryland 6:30 P.M., arrived in Canada 11 1/2 hours later. When we arrived, no one awake. Finally had breakfast at Will and Effie's, then to Gananoque for shopping. Approx. 11 A.M. arrived Pine Island. Water level as low as in late fall. Water temp.

48, barometer rising at 29.6, air temp. 55, day sunny, wind from west and very hard.

"May 25. Dawn fair and clear. Wind westerly not so hard. Barometer falling at 29.7. At 11:30 A.M., slight cirrus overcast, saw terns, and we think there are baby eel flies. (The local name for shadflies.) We readied the boats for painting. There seems to be a lot of mosquitoes. Water temp. in morning 50; in noon, 51. Air temp. in morning 62, in noon, 68. Went to Will and Effie's to bring boat junk back; gas tank and funnel broken. Water level 2 3/4 feet below dock height. We acquired licenses and Daddy caught first fish. It got away, though, and he tried again. Then *Chris caught and landed the first fish to be landed.*

"May 26. Dawn warm with gray skies and little if any wind. Water temp. 51 in morning, air 64, barometer falling at 29.4. We caught seven bass, none under 1 1/2 lbs., and two pike, 4 lbs. apiece. Rain in afternoon in gusts, but clearing later on. The late evening temp. is the same as early morning."

Reading those entries now is to see dawn red on a steel river; to be tired again from the long drive and to have still to drive to a store thirteen miles away before going out into a rising wind on cold water; to remember that you always find something broken in the spring that had not been broken when you put it away in the fall. It is to see at dawn a small scientist in pajamas tap the glass, peer at the sky, and pad off barefoot down the still-dark hall to walk down the stairs into the morning, and, leaving footprints in the dew on the gray-painted dock, to drop a little metal thermometer on a string into the sullen river. It is to feel again in your wrist and arm the sudden heavy tug of something in the depths; to see at last the big, dark-backed fish coming toward the dock three feet down, only to turn arrowing away toward the weeds; to feel the weight of him speeding in the secret river as the line pours wetly off the reel; to be tense with wonder—and then, nothing. But you were glad to have seen the fish and to know that there were fish still in the river; in a curious way glad to have lost him and then happier still in the exultation of the small boy who landed his fish while you lost yours.

"May 27," Chris reported, "dawn 54 with gray skies and heavy west wind. Barometer steady. Water temp. 50. Mother, Vicky, Magsy went to the Bay while Chris painted his boat and Daddy worked. Air temp. at noon is 60. Chris finished painting the hull of his boat and Daddy applied first coat to his tub. Baked pike for supper!

"May 28. Dawn cold and gloomy with changing wind. Barometer rising. Air temp. 48. Will said it was going to freeze tonight. Agnes will do our wash.

"May 29. Dawn beautiful. Barometer rising. Temp. about 70, water temp. 53. We chopped wood. After that, *Magsy & Chris went swimming!* Breeze from west. *Chris' boat launched!* Daddy's boat brought around to boathouse so that she would be out of the bugs."

Between the lines lie rocks and shoals. The immediate concern, on the day of arrival, was for the level of the river. A low water year was promised, which meant that while the river would not be full of floating debris (as it would be in a high-water spring that floats logs and brush from the banks), you must remember that there will be less water over the shoals and so give wider berth to certain rocks and islands. The log tells a tale of familiar bases touched, of anticipated pleasures re-experienced, of labor divided. The women wrapped in parkas and blankets wallow off in wind-driven spray to shop in Alexandria Bay for the canned and packaged foods that are all there is to buy at this time of year, while the boy in blue jeans, sweatshirt, and gloves stirs paint beside an outboard hull upside down on the dock and the father sits in a small bare room at the head of the island blowing on blue fingers to warm them sufficiently to type. The boy takes his chance that the air temp., as he puts it, will go above 50 so that the paint will stick. He must run this risk because it is necessary to have boats in the water if you live on an island. The man goes to his typewriter because, whatever the weather, if he does not do his work there will not be an island. The luck runs well; the chores are done; the weather warms enough to hold the paint; and after a day at the typewriter the man emerges to give the other boat a first coat. At night there is the first reward of eating a fish caught from your dock, stuffed and baked and basted with white wine. If Will said it would freeze, then against the chill of a frosty night there was a great blaze in the fireplace in the evening and a need to chop wood next day.

The water was always cold in spring, and we used the children as a sort of litmus paper. If they dived into the river and came out blue, Margaret and I did not go in. If they came out pink, we waited for the water to warm a bit more. If they came out the same color they were before they jumped off the dock, then we would edge into the river ourselves. But 53 degrees! So the log says, and so it must be true. Granted that children like to be wet and uncomfortable and that they have a metabolism that permits them to stay for hours in water that is too cold to allow a more human being to survive for more than fifteen minutes, it is still hard to believe that naked children bounced happily in and out of the river while we stood chill in woolen sweaters and trousers on the cold gray boards. The children took a different point of view, one that perhaps combined pride and masochism but was represented as bravura and delight. In any case, they took to the river like otters; they could hardly wait for the first swim; and looking back, I now recall that the magic number for them was 52. As soon as the water reached that temperature, in they went, turning a gleeful blue.

The log that spring notes that we went to the sand-banks to fill Victoria's sandbox. The dunes marked the shore of an old epiric sea—they are part of the same formation you will see at Gary, Indiana, complete with sand burrs. We would go there each spring to load buckets, for after Victoria stopped serving us cookies and pies made of wet sand and ferns there was still a need to keep sand in buckets as fire extinguishers in boats and on the island. But we also went to the sandbanks because it was a familiar pleasure to make a trip through remembered waterways and to lie on hot sand in the sun.

There was always an early trip to the Indian as well. The Indian could (and can) be found hiding beneath an overhanging rock on a cliff face, near the water's edge—

complete with his bark canoe, bow and arrows, and feathered headdress. Years ago he had been hotly pursued along the top of those cliffs, and he jumped his horse from the top of them. No one knows what happened to his horse, on which he had had the foresight to carry his canoe. So the horse is gone. On the way of his long fall, however, the Indian got out his box of war-paints, which he always carried, and painted a picture of himself falling. There you see him, bow and arrows in his hands, feathers waving, with the canoe still falling after him. One spring we repainted him, while Margaret told the story. She knew it better than anyone else, having made it up when, as a child, she painted the Indian there.

Elsewhere in North America that year summer may have come, but on the fifth of June there was a heavy north wind and it was 42 degrees. The river was cooling rather than warming. The next day there was "thunderstorm in the evening, everyone scared stiff. The screens blew down. No fish, believe it or not!" A week later the air was freezing: 32 degrees. On June 24 the log reports, "Terrific gale. Barometer fell to 29.0. Water rose (because of west wind) 1 foot. The few boats on the river pitched beautifully. Davidsons are due, later found out it was Hurricane Audrey."

Here I must say there is no such thing as good weather or bad weather. This is because weather is a fact, like a shelf of stone in a dirt road is a fact. The stone is neither good nor bad, it is simply there, and since it is too vast for you to break or move, what matters is your decision as to what to do about it. You might decide to turn back to try to find some other road; you might accept its existence and look for the best way to surmount it. It is your decision that will prove good or bad, but not the stone. With respect to the weather, our decision was to enjoy whatever it was, within the limits of prudence. We looked forward to the first real storms quite as much as we looked forward to the first walk back country to get eggs at the Wallace farm, to the first trip to the sandbanks, to the first sight of the Indian and the feel of the strike of the first fish. This was not making a virtue of necessity; there is glory and excitement in a storm, particularly in one that scares you stiff, as Chris put it. We know one woman on a neighboring island who hides in a closet whenever there is a thunderstorm, which is not really so much an act of fear as one of communion. Our rather similar action is to watch the darkness come across the river. The wheeling terns, speeding ahead of the darkness over the green waves, turn a lovely, incredible white against the blue-ink clouds as they catch the last of the light. Our excitement rises with the wind. "Did you see *that!*" we exclaim to one another when lightning strikes so close that you can hear the *pfft* of it before the crash that rattles the dishes. We run about with towels to stop the leaks along the window frames and under the hall door and glory in the way the waves break upon the island stones.

I said that spring came late that year, and while this seems true enough, the log entries for other years assure me that the weather was not unusual and that spring departed fairly close to schedule.

Whether spring came early or late, it always seemed to end on the Fourth of July. This was in part due to the return of the first summer people. In early spring in the Thousand Islands, you have the river to yourself. If you see another boat on the water, you know whose boat it is, who is in it, where he is going, and why he is going there. You wave to him, and he waves to you, and it is not just the sort of waving that people in speedboats do. It is a greeting. Late in the spring the first tour boats appear half empty, then gradually fill. The fishermen from Pennsylvania return to such cabins as the Hucks and Chub Massey keep for them, and many of the boats are strange. But beginning with the Fourth of July, the summer residents of islands return, and recognizing the way a mahogany speedboat sits on the water a mile away, you say, "I see the Gilberts are back." We have lived on the river for twenty years and have never met the Gilberts, who live on an island two miles from ours, but we know their boats and where they live, and presumably they know our boats and our island, and so we wave when we see one another's boats on the river. This is not a greeting but a mutually understood signal of recognition that a season is about to begin. Before it does, however, spring ends in fireworks.

There was always a great excitement about the fireworks. We always buy them from a particular fireworks shop in Gananoque, where they can be bought all year long, but we buy them only for the Fourth of July, entrusting their selection to the children. Five dollars is always the limit, and two purchases are mandatory. There must be sparklers enough for everyone and one Burning Schoolhouse. Within those limits grave decisions must be made as to the relative values of Roman candles and firecrackers. You can buy a good many small ones of each, or a few larger, gaudier and louder ones for the same money. Then, too, there are individual tastes to consider. Meanwhile, everything in the shop looks wonderful, and all the most wonderful-looking things cost more than you can afford. Buying five dollars' worth of fireworks can take a splendid hour of imagination, anticipation, and shrewd debate.

The night is likely to be cold on the Fourth of July, so cold that we have seldom shot off fireworks without wearing parkas. The river is usually so cold that Margaret and I have not gone for our first swim. There is the long wait after supper till it is dark enough, for there is a long light in the north country, but when the night comes it somehow always seems to be clear and without a moon. As soon as they were old enough to be entrusted with the work, the children would push out in a boat to the swimming dock with a bucket of sand to serve as a base for the Roman candles. Of course, a fuse always burned out and had to be relighted, dangerously. You jumped aside from the brightening flame before, with a pop and a woosh, the red, white, and blue fireballs shot from the slender tube to describe arcs high above the dark glistening water. The best of the candles was the kind that sent brilliant-tailed comets into the sky. After the candles, strings of Chinese firecrackers, held on fishing rods, exploded over the water; then there would be sparklers on the dock, and everyone wrote his name in fire in the night. The little spitting fires lighted the drifting gray powder-smelling smoke of the candles and the firecrackers. Just before the sparklers burned out, you threw them as far up and out over the water as you could, and they would be comets, too, that, if you judged it right, winked out just before they fell with a hiss in the river. The last act was the Burning Schoolhouse. The fire started on the first story, then flames shot out the windows while everyone cheered. There she goes! we would say when the roof fell in. The larger flames would lick up, and we all felt an enormous satisfaction when, as we said, she burned right down to the ground. So much for education. Summer could now begin, and, in a strange way, summer always did begin on the fifth of July. The early green leaves were darker and fuller, the weather turned fine and stayed that way, the summer people were back, the river warmed, and there was not only swimming by day but skinny-dipping at night. Spring had gone somewhere else, to waken another world.

8

When you live and work alone with your family on an island, the choices you make are increasingly your own, and others may find them eccentric—as did a New York editor who came to visit us. When I showed him the playhouse we had made for our daughters and explained that the little building had once housed a power plant, he was horrified. He thought I had lowered the resale value of the island by doing away with electricity, whereas I felt that by dispensing with the noise and smell of the engines and the glare of electric light, we had enhanced our standard of living and thereby increased the value of the island.

The editor was even more horrified to learn that we

lived not only without telephone, radio, and television but also without magazines and the daily *New York Times.* How could I as a writer afford to be so completely out of touch with all that was going on? I tried to explain that there was no need to be in daily touch with contemporary events, that it does not really matter whether you read the Sunday *Times* on Sunday, next Thursday or next month, because the important news will keep if it really is important. This did not satisfy the editor. He thought we were trying to escape from the world.

It was a thought that applies well enough to guests or summer people who come to the islands to spend a time in the sun away from responsibilities and think about nothing. It is difficult for them, as it was for the editor, to imagine anyone living and working on an island. They can all imagine living on one but not working there, because work, to most people, is something they do together with others away from home. They talk, for example, about children leaving home or college to go out into the real world—as if home were not one real thing and college another. The real world to them implies a kind of jungle through which they must cut their way like so many members of an expedition, wary of sloughs, quicksands, predators, and savages. To live outside the jungle seems a kind of cheating.

Actually, no one lives outside the jungle, and there are more kinds of jungles than city people may imagine; but it was certainly true that the island's demands were turning our attention inward and reordering our sense of values, as may be seen in our purchase of a boat.

That occurred one day during the second spring we

lived on the island. Chuck Handley, Will's great-nephew, came to say he had found a boat for sale upriver on the American side. He knew, as we now had learned, how inadequate two small outboards would be for us and how essential it was to have a boat that could live in any weather. Chuck was not so much trying to sell a boat as he was looking out for us.

The instant we saw her we knew there was no need to look further. She was twenty-one feet long, beamy and deep-hulled—a copper-riveted, round-bottomed, lapstrake open launch with a 60-horsepower Gray engine amidships. She had been built by Hutchinson in Alexandria Bay in 1935 by men who took care and pride in their work, and every board in her was Philippine red narra. She carried a rack for fishing rods, a live-bait well, and a hoist for her anchor. When the children stood on her floorboards, the gunwales were higher than their waists. They would be safe in her.

She needed varnish, and there were still war numbers painted on her sides. These blocked and shaded numbers a yard high were put there by government order during the war, apparently to distinguish her from a German submarine or from God knew what else the government might have imagined the invading enemy would use to fish from. Before revarnishing, we would have to take her down to the wood to get the shadow of those painted numbers out. Did she leak? Were there any rotten boards or knees? What was the state of the old Gray, and how much did she cost?

Chuck swore she was ready to go—and Will, taking up the floorboards to examine the dry bilge, looking into the forepeak hatch, and feeling beneath the gasoline tank astern, agreed that she was.

"She's a dandy," Will muttered to me. "I'd take her if I was you."

The price was thirteen hundred dollars, which we did not have, but which was a fair price, so we bought her. In the easy river way of doing business, we shook hands with the owner and drove home to the island in the boat we already called the *Margaret*. We would find the money later, and I had an idea where to look for it.

I was at this time paying premiums on a life-insurance policy which would, when paid up, be worth five thousand dollars but which then had a cash surrender value of fifteen hundred. I cashed the policy. Buying the *Margaret* seemed to me a more realistic way of insuring all our lives. We put the rest of the money into still another form of insurance: We replaced those potential fire hazards in the kitchen—the coal-oil stove, refrigerator and water heater—with bottle-gas equipment and bought a lawnmower engine to pump water.

From the very beginning of our life on the island we began to think in terms peculiar to our situation, and perhaps it was high time that we did. After all, we had three young children, and if you are going to have children, your first and immediate obligation is to give them as best you can the means to survive in the world in which they find themselves. The only thing you can give them is yourself. Americans have been accused of undue pediacentricity, but it might be more correct to arraign them on charges of improper pediacentricity to the extent that they want to give their children (as they say) everything that everyone else has. However this may be, I think that any family ought to devote its major attention to itself, which is certainly easier to do on an island than in a city which separates a family by age and sex and assigns each member a kind of nameplate to wear in an appropriate crowd of coeval strangers.

Looking back on the first five island years, I am astonished to discover, from evidence in the log, how self-contained we were. Our social occasions were almost exclusively confined to the family, which included Bob, his wife Kate and their children, Bocy and Sally. The cousins got along wonderfully well; the boys were the same age, as were young Margaret and Sally. Will's grandson Donny, who was a year older than the boys, joined in the swimming, fishing, and games, and they all made whatever room was necessary for small Victoria. The group was now and then enlarged by two other families who came separately to vacation on Fancy Rock, the island closest to our own. We met them through our children. The first was a Montreal family: Gordon Davidson, his wife, Peter, and their children, Peter Gordon and Andrea, who were about the ages of our son and older daughter. The names were a bit confusing at first, as was their status. We thought they were the owners of the island, for we had been told Fancy Rock belonged to a blonde Hollywood actress. But it turned out that Peter had been a model, not an actress, and that they spent a fortnight on the island in summer thanks to the kindness of their friends, the Rahes, who were the owners. It was Joan Rahe who had been the actress, a brunette one from Broadway, not Hollywood, and she and her husband

Roderic and their three sons came to the river in July. Their older boy was also of an age with Chris and Bocy; the younger ones were Victoria's contemporaries and immediately became her constant companions. Once, when everyone's visits overlapped on a weekend, Donny Slate, seeing all the Bodine, Keats, Davidson and Rahe children on the island at once, said, "Gee, the whole kids are here!"

However many children there were on the island, they were wholly there, and we were wholly involved with them. We did the simple chores in common, for everyone could see the need for doing them and helped to the extent he could. Our simple pleasures were like-wise shared. I am sure that the reasons for our getting along so well were that everyone could play a part in what was done and that the children were at that stage of life when they wanted to do things with us. These circumstances were not planned but quite natural and spontaneous. We were the only people we knew, and so we did what there was to do. We fished, swam, and taught ourselves to sail, water ski, and use the Aqualung. We would go to the mainland to walk two miles inland, through pastures filled with boulders, hay and wildflow-ers, to buy eggs at Jim and Hazel Wallace's farm. They were an elderly childless couple, and whenever children came to their farm Jim would come in from field or barn to enjoy their visit with Hazel in the kitchen. "Kids to Hazels and got scared of the cows," a log entry reads. "Hazel wasn't home anyway because it was Election Day in Canada." Of course we would not have known that it was, living as we did in a world where time had to do only with such matters as whether it was time to go for a picnic.

The picnics took place elsewhere, off our island, but not in the outside world. We went instead to five little islands that lie in a lonely and shoal-filled stretch of the river seven miles downstream. We almost never saw other boats, although the water there is a fine fishing ground. The islands were a group of ocher-colored lichened stones covered with summer grasses, fire-cone pines, sumacs, birches, and blueberries. There were no houses. The only residents were a family of bald eagles whose enormous nest was built in a wind-twisted pine. Drawing near the islands, watching for shoals, we had the very pleasant and mysterious feeling of being the first explorers of a small, desolate, and beautiful new world of our own.

This feeling was enhanced by the landing we made. At the foot of the largest island was a deep cove at the base of a cliff; all other shorelines were shelving rock. The cove provided a protected anchorage for *Margaret*. Chris and his cousin Bocy would come alongside in an outboard motorboat to take from us the picnic gear and ferry it to a beach of rock onto which the outboard could be skidded on boards brought for this purpose. Having unloaded the gear, they would return for their fellow explorers waiting in *Margaret*.

There was driftwood to gather and a fireplace to build of island stones, but first there was the island to examine. The boys raced ahead and disappeared, while the girls, of a more practical turn of mind, followed slowly and carefully, paper cups in hand, searching for wildflowers and blueberries. The wildflowers were for me. I always maintained, when the subject of going on a picnic was broached, that man took his first step toward civilization when he decided to go indoors to eat, even if only into a cave. Pretending to believe me, the girls would always bring a small end table, no larger than a stand for a plate and a glass, and a folding canvas chair. In turn, I always pretended to be astonished, when the picnic was ready, to find a table reserved for me, spread with a paper serviette and set with a cup of flowers, so that I could sit down to a meal in a civilized manner— while everyone else sat with plates in their laps happily uncomfortable on boat-cushioned stones.

The picnics in our private world were never spoiled by the weather. Once we were caught in a thunderstorm just as the corn, roasting in its shucks in the ashes, was nearly done, but this disaster added a quality of adventure to the occasion, for an adventure is something whose course and end cannot be foreseen.

We would leave the picnic islands at night. Once, during the long, slow trip upriver, the night was black everywhere save in the north. That quarter pulsated with shafts and waves of pale-green and dull-red fire; hanging draperies formed and changed and vanished, and new shapes of light appeared. We would have been content if that night had continued forever.

"What do you *do* all day on an island?" a woman once asked Margaret.

The question was asked in a tone of horror that implied a fear of lonely, empty, mindless time. Margaret never answered it. She was all eyes and ears all day long, no matter how placid or artless our activity, because when children are small, cliffs and water can be dangerous. This was perfectly well understood by the Bodines, the Davidsons, the Rahes, and no doubt by everyone else who ever raised a family on water. The dangerous aspect of the river was one reason, apart from all others, why we and our children were so much together. There was safety in numbers. We all looked after one another and acquired in the process what islanders call river eyes. We all followed the rule *no one ever swims alone,* not even adults, and the children had to wear lifejackets on the dock and in the boat, until they could swim at least as far as our neighboring island, Fancy Rock. In our first five years on the island, there was never a year in which someone did not have to be pulled out of the river, and one year it was Donny Slate.

We and the Bodines were talking with Will and Effie at their mainland cottage when we heard my daughter Margaret shrieking, and we all raced down to the dock to find Donny in the water. Another year, a guest's infant child scrambled out of our boat before it had been moored, and before I knew what had happened my wife was in the water, clothes, boots, coat, wrist watch and all, together with a boat cushion to buoy herself and the howling baby. The rules required Victoria to wear a lifejacket whenever she was out of doors, and she liked this so much that she even took a lifejacket to bed with her. But once when we were all on the dock together with all the Davidsons and their children, Donny suddenly said, "Victoria's on the bottom!" This was not entirely true; she was coming to the surface. Somehow or other, although all of us were within a yard or so of the little inflated bathing pool in which the baby played on the dock, she had left her play pool, got out of her lifejacket, and fallen off the dock. Thereafter, we mounted a kind of rotating guard over her.

A need of constant vigilance by no means diminished our pleasure of the river, nor was it a price we paid. Rather, to be vigilant was to be responsible, and it was important for the children to learn that life is the sum of the responsibilities you accept—a point much easier to understand on an island than anywhere else, because on an island the relationship of one thing to another is at once simple and transparently obvious. We wanted each child to be able to operate each of the outboard motorboats and the *Margaret* as soon as possible, because there could be an occasion when someone would have to go to the mainland to seek help for an incapacitated parent or (less dramatically) to run an errand while everyone else was otherwise occupied. Of course the children wanted to run the boats anyway, and the lessons began as soon as each was old enough to sit on our laps with a hand on the tiller, but need, as well as pleasure, was always in their minds. They were not allowed to go out alone in boats, however, until they demonstrated their competence at swimming, in handling the boats, and their knowledge of rocks, shoals, and the International Rules of the Road. This made sense to the children, as did our painting the old, slow cypress outboard motorboat a brilliant scarlet, visible a mile or more away. When they left the island they were always to say where they intended to go, upriver or down, and when they would return.

They did not object to this; they, too, would be worried if a boat were overdue and they would want to know where to begin to look for it. They took to boats and their implicit responsibilities as eagerly as they took to water, and by the time Victoria was in third grade she was going alone in the scarlet outboard on errands to Rockport.

By that time she was of course some years out of her lifejacket. The end of the lifejacket came at one summer's end when it occurred to me to wonder at the weight of the thing she had been swimming in all season. I put it over the side to test its buoyance, and it sank like an anvil. Victoria swore she couldn't swim without it, but now that it was clear to her that she had been swimming with several pounds of dead weight on her back, she soon paddled off to Fancy Rock without it and moved on to boats.

If we lived out of touch with all that was going on, as the New York editor put it, the same could be said of our children, who lived entirely apart from whatever fads and entertainments were bemusing children in the mainland world. They necessarily devised their own entertainments. Victoria built a house of towels, clothesline, and the front steps' rail, and here she had her nation. She wanted customs duty every time you passed through. When the two Rahe boys came to play, they were citizens of her country. More than this, they were such good friends that one of them paid Victoria a small boy's ultimate compliment: "We don't think of you as a girl," he said. The older children had a different point of view. Chris, Bocy, and their friend Donny were Indians in breechclouts and charcoal warpaint, or pirates, but they were most often fishermen. Girls were excluded from the boys' company, but, involved in their own affairs, they never noticed this. Our daughter Margaret and her cousin Sally invented an elaborate theater. They would spend an entire day working out a story not without a quality of drama, make sets and costumes, and in the evening when all was ready invite us into our living room, selling tickets at the door. When we were seated, the curtain would rise on their production. The actors were their dolls and stuffed animals and, once in a while, Victoria.

A danger in the kind of life we were living is the gathering feeling that the rest of the world is not only irrelevant but a place to be shunned. If such a feeling does grow on you, you are liable to be disabused of it by forces beyond anyone's control. One experience, beyond all others, assured us of our common humanity —although at the same time it demanded our self-reliance.

It occurred one fall night, a night all fair and warm with a moon riding in the silent, windless sky. There was a curious quality of vague apprehension in the air. The barometer had been dropping all day long, and in the evening Christopher looked at it again. "It says hurricane," he solemnly reported. We made the usual joke about the barometer being broken. Hurricanes, after all, ought not come to the St. Lawrence River. Still, a falling barometer means wind to come, and before going to bed we tied each boat four ways in the boat slips. Because it was warm and still, we did not close the windows and doors.

We came awake feeling the house shuddering, hearing doors banging. The pines were roaring. Below us were the sounds of ropes humming taut and wood screeching as the surging boats sought to tear the cleats from the slip docks. The bright moon showed water curiously flat. There were waves, but the booming east wind tended to flatten them and to shove the entire river west out of its bed. We flew out of bed naked—it was no time for niceties—and, carrying flashlights, went at once down to the boat slips to fix six more lines to *Margaret* and two more to each of the outboards while the house groaned over our heads. I cannot remember rain. People died in torrential rains and floods in Toronto that night, but on the island we had moonlight and a wind that rose and filled the world with sound and kept rising to higher powers. Having experienced a typhoon in the Pacific, I was fully aware of what wind could do, and it was only too easy to envision the boathouse torn from the island and sent collapsing into the river. So long as the wind remained in the east, we would be spared its full force because a cliff on that side of the island provided something of a lee. But the wind was deafening and increasing, and it was all we could do to climb the staircase against it.

Finding in excitement a strength we would not otherwise possess, we managed to close doors and windows against the wind. That done, we dressed. The older children, blown awake, had both gone from their bedrooms to look after their small sister. Christopher shouted that the barometer was not broken. He was pleased to be in a hurricane because he had never been in one before.

There was a tearing crack in the night and a dreadful concussive thud. A great pine, more than a hundred feet tall, had fallen on the path to the head of the island, and now I feared that the huge trees close to the boathouse would also topple; if they did, they would fall into our bedrooms. We had no storm cellar. To huddle in the lee at the foot of a great boulder would make sense, but to go outside would be foolhardy. The safest place seemed to be around the living-room fireplace, for the hearth was built on a cement foundation that went down to mother rock, and it was the one place in the house farthest from where the trees would fall, if they did. We dragged mattresses into the living room.

The children wanted to know what to do, and since there was nothing else we could do, I suggested we all go back to sleep. We composed ourselves on the mattresses on the floor that creaked as the house moved in the wind, but Victoria was too excited to be still. She kept starting off somewhere, and I had at last to anchor her down by throwing a leg across her.

Of course none of us slept. It was, however, necessary for purposes of morale to pretend that we did. Hours later, it seemed, the wind stopped as suddenly as it had come. The silence was appalling. We looked out on moonlit water that still moved with a vast surge, but we could not see what damage might have been done to Fancy Rock. The Rahes' house gleamed in the pale light; it still had its roof, but the shingles were standing like bristles. The barometer was steady, at the lowest point I had ever seen, and believing completely in it now, I said we were in the eye of the hurricane and that we could expect it all back again, this time blowing out of the west, which would have the virtue that, if the trees fell now, they would fall away from the house, and if the house was blown over, it would at least be blown ashore. During the calm we checked the boats. They were unharmed, but the knots in the ropes were so tight we had to use a marlin spike to work them apart in order to retie the boats. If at some last resort we had to chance using a boat, we would have to cut her lines. I remembered there was a knife in each baitbox.

When the west wind came the flat side of the house took the force of it. Waves piled over our docks, and we could hear an underwater timber working loose from a crib and thumping against stavings in the boat slips. The noise of wind and water and the noises of the house went on and on in the night until some time in the earliest morning hours when the wind at last let go of us, and we fell asleep.

Later that morning we learned that Hurricane Hazel had passed over us. If we had listened to a radio or read a newspaper or talked with someone on the mainland, we might have known that such a storm had been doing great damage in the eastern United States for some days and that it was headed for the river with undiminished force. I cannot say what we would have done had we been warned. We might have gone to the mainland to moor our boats in a protected cove behind Will and Effie's house and spent the night there. More likely, we would have disbelieved the storm warnings, much as we disregarded the barometer, telling ourselves the hurricane would spend itself before reaching the river, or secretly thinking that damage in storms is what happens to other people.

We never learned how hard the wind blew. At some point in the hurricane, after registering 110 miles an hour, the anemometer blew off the roof of the Alexandria Bay weather station. We did see damage everywhere, and everyone on the mainland had his story to tell of power lines down, barns collapsed, cattle killed, and boats sunk. The first, east wind had pushed a kind of tidal wave ashore in Rockport, which poured over the transoms of all the boats moored in Ed Andress' boat slips. All the boats but one, the *Dorcas,* sank at their moorings. When the storm came the old man had summoned men to help him, and they had stayed up all night to save that one boat—a beautiful, antique naphtha launch whose cabin roof, with its scalloped edges, looked for all the world like a surrey's; whose paneled cabin had crystal flower vases swung in brightly polished brass gimbals. While Ed did not own the *Dorcas,* she belonged to him more than any boat did, and he and his men worked in her, pumping, while that wall of water, built by the wind, piled over her transom. They rigged lines in such a way that cleats would not be pulled out of the rails; and, since this took all their effort, they had none to spare for other craft. Now in the morning they were beginning to raise the sunken boats.

People told us they had thought of us in the night. When that blow came across the water, they said, we hoped you were all right out there on the island. How did you make out? We said we had been lucky to have lost only one of the pines, but the house had a bad list to it.

We were told that a line could be bent around a corner post, and, with a block and tackle pulling on one of the surviving pines, the house could be pulled back into plumb and shimmed to stay there. If there was underwater damage, the house could be jacked up from a barge and new timbers fitted beneath it. Things could have been worse, people said, and then they told us about the people drowned in Toronto. We were sure thinking of you, they said, and at that point the storm at last came home to us.

We had not been thinking about them.

To be sure, we had been busy, but so had the men who had worked to save a boat that belonged to none of them and who, while standing in wind and water, had hoped the folks on the islands would be all right.

Evidently, self-sufficiency could be carried just so far, and the world beyond the island was neither remote nor totally irrelevant. It had its legitimate claims upon us, and one of these pertained to the children. In those earliest years upon the river we stayed late into the fall. The seasons did not always keep time with the calendar, and we could see no reason to leave blue water and warm sunlight just because the calendar said it was Labor Day and all the children in Maryland would have to return to school. We selfishly stayed where we were, but with respect to others than ourselves we entered our older children in Rockport's elementary school—Christopher in the fifth grade, his sister Margaret in the second.

School began on September 1, no matter whether the day was designed for swimming rather than for arithmetic, and it began at eight in the morning and kept till four in the afternoon. When one of the two teachers rang the bell, the boys lined up at the door for boys and the girls at the one for girls and filed into the school's two rooms and remained standing till their teachers said good morning and told them to be seated. Each room held four rows of desks; each row constituted one grade. Grades one through four were taught in one room, five through eight in the other. At recess, the boys and girls played in their separate yards. When cold weather came, the coal stoves were fired and tended by the boys, and there would be a hot lunch. Everyone would bring a potato to roast in the flue.

Each morning our children would set off with their lunchboxes, rulers, and pencils in the scarlet outboard that became the Little Red School Bus, with Margaret as crew obedient in the bow and her brother the captain at the tiller astern. They would land at Ed Huck's boatyard, more than a mile across channel, and walk the mile uphill through pastures to school. The first day was a disaster for our daughter.

"They write on the blackboard," she explained, "and I can't read writing because I learned printing. I can't understand the teacher—" she had a Scottish burr —"and I don't know the words to 'God Save the Queen'!"

Christopher took a brother's view of his sister. He said he *liked* school, because when the teacher wasn't teaching his grade he could listen and learn what she was teaching the others.

"And the teacher hits kids on the head if they do something wrong," Margaret said. "She hits them with a ruler!"

"The teacher doesn't hit me," Christopher said. "She only hits the kids who do something wrong."

His sister gave him a sisterly look.

"She hit me on the head today," said Donny Slate, who was visiting.

"What did you do wrong?" I asked.

"I didn't do nothing," Donny said. "But I'll probably do something tomorrow."

Homework began with the beginning of school, and in Christopher's grade the homework in English that night required each child to write an essay that, in his words, would retell a story from the Bible. Since Christopher's reading had not as yet included this valuable work, he sat himself down by lamplight and began with the begats. "What does begat mean?" he wanted to know. Hours later he had come upon a text that had real meaning for him: the miracle of the loaves and fishes. We saved his essay because it began: "Jesus crossed over the Sea of Galilee with a great mob of disciples. They all went up a hill and sat down. Then one of the disciples came to Him and said, 'Jesus Christ, how are we going to feed the mob?' "

The Canadian school was very different from the one in Maryland, and so was the attitude of the children. We had seen there was a difference between man's work and woman's work in the Rockport community. It now appeared that going to school was the children's work and that everyone, including the children themselves, expected them to work as hard at it as their parents did at their respective tasks. It was a school that accepted the fact of failure. If a child could not meet the standards of one grade, it was silly to expect him to succeed in the next. He was therefore kept back until he did master the work of that grade—if necessary, until school-leaving age. In the Canadian system, the child who spent three years in the seventh grade was not unusual. Nor was he condemned. It was simply recognized that he would have to work harder if he intended to get into the eighth. The amount and quality of the homework demanded was a welcome surprise to us.

Among the children, we noticed a quality of friendliness. There were no fights in the schoolyard. When it occurred to the eighth-grade boys to have an athletic program, about which neither of the lady teachers knew much, they borrowed books on athletics from the Gananoque public library. They laid out a track, dug jumping pits, made a high-jump standard, and otherwise provided for track and field events and taught themselves—using the older boys as tutors for the younger. There was a feeling of community about this school, no doubt because everyone in it came from the Rockport area. There was no such feeling in Maryland, very likely because the children there were strangers to one another, oddly met in a kind of impersonal factory to which they had all been brought by buses from homes or communities many miles apart. The little red brick schoolhouse with its disciplinarians and its coal stoves had its limitations, but then so did the multimillion-dollar Maryland factory with its big new fieldhouse and splendid parking lot. The shortcomings of the latter lay in the area of academic achievement. In Canada, our children learned of the Crusades, of European history, discovered that there had been Europeans in America for hundreds of years before the Pilgrims made their dour landing and that there were cathedrals and universities in Mexico and Peru a century before Bostonians built houses. When we returned to Maryland as winter came, the children could rest on their academic oars and wait for their Maryland class to catch up to them. And since this never occurred by May, we could simply take them out of that Maryland school and return to the island.

It would seem, in the case of the children's Canadian schooling, they entered a world different from any they had known and which they certainly had not suspected to exist.

Likewise, the apparently self-contained and self-centered life that Margaret and I had been living on the island was not without its own reference to external reality. I have said that I worked on the island, but the point escaped those whose employment was so different from mine that they thought (as one of them said) I did not have a job. It also escaped the New York editor who thought we were out of touch with the world simply because the world he inhabited, and which he thought was all-important, happened not to be in touch with many others. When told, for example, that at least four million Americans subscribed to outdoor magazines, he tended to dismiss this fact as unimportant because he could not imagine serious men taking fishing seriously.

But the subscribers could, and so could the editors of outdoor magazines, and so could I. Indeed, fishing was quite important to me, because during the early years of our life on the island our fishing trips, which we hugely enjoyed, also enabled us to live on the island. We fished for more than fun, and one of those trips was almost no fun at all.

I had been asked to write an article on catching muskellunge. The editor of the outdoor magazine wanted me to catch a muskie myself and have pictures taken to establish the article's authenticity. This was fair enough, but muskellunge are neither rare nor common in the St. Lawrence River. A good fisherman can spend twenty years fishing for them without a strike, whereas another can fish the same water and take one every day, boating muskies ranging from fifteen to more than fifty pounds. Ralph Peck, the game warden, felt that I would have a chance if Margaret and I fished every day for a week on the Forty Acre Shoal that lies between Clayton, New York, and Gananoque, Ontario.

We arranged for Victoria to stay with Will and Effie during the day while our older children were at school, and at seven o'clock the first morning Margaret and I arrived at the passage between Thwartway and Grindstone Islands, soaked and chilled by a light but steady cold rain. As we came through the passage, with the *Margaret* slowed and the big baits trolled astern, there we saw what we had come to hunt. It was lying awash in the rain, the top of the tail breaking water, looking at us with an eye big as half a dollar, curious, perhaps, but certainly uncaring. We stared, not speaking, as that heavy, blotched-silver shape slid down beneath the rain—down toward the shoals three fathoms below.

"Your bait will go right past him," I muttered.

"Just keep the way you're going," she said in a voice as low.

Not till we had gone a hundred yards did we give up hope of a strike. We caught nothing that day and nothing the next. It rained every day that week and every day we spent on that water, fishing from seven to noon, resting for an hour in the cold wet, fishing again till four when the children were coming home from school and the light was beginning to fail. We made our daily lunch on fried chicken, a bottle of Canadian whisky, and a one-pound chocolate bar, needing the fat and sugar because of the dank chill. Sometimes we had what we thought must have been strikes, because when we reeled in there were no bottom weeds on the gang hooks of the big plugs. Once we knew we had had a strike because the wooden bait was toothmarked and splintered. Sometimes we would foul bottom, which was momentarily exciting because a big muskellunge hits so hard you think you must have struck a rock. Once I had a wild time, trying to reel while my line was carried heavily and erratically all over the river, both of us certain that the fish was not much larger than Moby Dick, until at last I landed three hundred feet of someone's Monel wire line —together with its trolling plug and what was left of a broken reel.

We were by this time fishing just a bit desperately, because we had invested a week's time, pounds of chocolate, several chickens, gallons of gasoline, and bottles of whisky in a literary speculation that would yield nothing unless we could produce a handsome photograph of the expert fisherman with his remarkable catch. From time to time we could see, across the gray water, the white splashes hooked fish made near boats a quarter mile away and hear the excited shouts of fishermen coming faintly through the rain. Worse, as we made one pass along the side of Thwartway Island, where we had seen the big fish on our first day, the boat following slowly along the path we had taken stopped to solve a problem. In that boat were Ralph Peck and his wife, enjoying an aquatic sort of bus driver's holiday, and the problem that Ralph was quickly and skillfully solving was how to gaff and land the splendid fish that had ignored our baits in favor of his. He held it up to show us, having to use two hands, and we wrenched on our smiles and croaked our congratulations.

The morning of the seventh day was all wrong for fishing. The wind was in the wrong quarter, the barometer was rising; it was bright and sunny after the week of rain. But Ralph had said if we fished all day for a week we would have a fish, so we decided to try one more time. It would be the last time for reasons of economy—and also because there is no pleasure in fishing to someone else's order. At ten in the morning I was fast to something that was neither bottom nor a bale of old wire. The heavy rod was alive and pumping, the line cutting swiftly this way and that through the sparkling waves. Whatever it was, was pulling like a colt in his first halter, next running like a bonefish, and in no way fighting and jump-

ing like a muskellunge. I wondered if by some chance I
had snagged a sturgeon of several hundred pounds.

We saw him at last near the boat, a silver ingot deep
in the cold clear water, and, seeing the boat, down he
went in a sort of inverse Immelmann turn. I fought the
rod tip up and stayed with the underwater acrobatics till
all I felt was a dead weight that I winched carefully toward the surface. Margaret stood nervously at the gunwale with the gaff.

She had never used a gaff before and wondered if
she was supposed to slip the hook in behind the gills.

"Just whack him with it anywhere you can," I told
her.

She doubted that she would be strong enough to
hold the fish, much less pull it over the *Margaret*'s side.
I told her we would figure all that out later—and meanwhile continued to reel until we could see the fish coming up from the depths, curiously immobile.

Margaret need not have worried. In the course of
those last acrobatics the fish had got so tangled in the
wire leader that he was trussed in it. Margaret simply
slipped the curved hook through two loops of wire. Nor
was there a problem about her bringing the fish into the
boat. It was easily the smallest muskellunge ever taken
from the Forty Acre Shoal—a fish just long enough to be
legal, weighing only eight pounds. But it was, after all,
a genuine muskellunge; we took pictures of each other
with the fish in and out of its wire lashings. Then, because there is a Thousand Island tradition that says if you
catch a muskie you must hoist a white flag and run
straight home, we improvised a flag. I peeled off the

layers of parka, wool sweater and wool shirt and shivered briefly. My T-shirt bravely flapping from a trolling rod, we made our proud way downriver, acknowledging the salutes of occasional fall fishermen. The next time we fished we would do it in our own time and in our own way and so enjoy our work. This had too nearly resembled a job.

Yet one island thing in some way relates to every other, and the muskellunge we caught that day served a purpose beyond the objective facts of life. The Davidsons came next day from Montreal to spend the Canadian Harvest Home holiday with us. Our baked muskellunge dominated the long oak table. It seemed appropriate to have this, together with the vegetables and fruits of the mainland harvest, on the day of Canadian Thanksgiving. After supper we stood on the porch and saw all the stars reflected in the still water below; we looked up from the stars in the water to the stars in the sky, and it was as if we were suspended at the center of the slowly circling galaxies.

We stayed late on the river that year. The children went into the back-country farms for pumpkins on Halloween, and on that day someone stole the clapper of the school bell. All the children told the teacher they were not going to enter the school till the bell rang. Our children went out in the *Margaret* wearing Halloween masks, racing alongside the last of the tour boats to dismay the tourists, and the pranks of the Canadian children were as artless, childish, and old-fashioned. There was no trick or treat; the Canadian children did not think in terms of blackmail.

There were river fogs that fall, and one of them closed around the children's scarlet boat just as it left our dock. It closed in so quickly and so thickly that we could not see them, nor they our island from two yards away. We tried to call them back, but they did not hear us over the sound of their outboard motor, and off they blundered into a kind of wet cotton batting. By good fortune they reached mainland. When they suddenly found the boat moving into a cat-o'-nine-tails marsh, Chris guessed it must be the one below the Hucks' boatyard and ran slowly upriver, keeping to the edge of the reeds, till the boatyard materialized before them. He was pleased with himself for having been able to cross the river when many a man would have been lost on it, but he never wanted to do a thing like that again.

We stayed on our island till milk froze in the kitchen and winds leaned on the island, scattering snow among the berry bushes. One morning of wind, icy waves and snow, I had to take the children across to school in the *Margaret*. They slipped on the ice on Rockport's town dock. Returning to the island, I found Victoria happily running over the snowy rocks barefoot. All she needed was a paper dress, a broom, and instructions to find strawberries. The sight was a bit too much when added to the ice in the sink and the ice water that struck your face when the *Margaret* entered a cross-wind chop in mid-channel. The season, I thought, had really come to an end; it was time we went south to Maryland for the winter.

In remembering these and other events of the earliest years of our life on our island, I cannot believe ours was a life of isolation. It is true that our attention turned inward upon ourselves, which gave a possibly elliptical turn to our thought, but our attention was not wholly self-directed. We were in touch with something—not with the great world, perhaps, but certainly with a real one of children, hurricanes, sky, work, fogs, school, fishing, and picnics. The island conditioned our responses, which, parochial as they may have seemed, were nonetheless responsible.

PART THREE

9

Summer takes forever to arrive and leaves you much too soon, but when you are together time has no beginning, middle, or end. The trees are in full leaf in a dozen shades of green, the grasses are luxuriant, there is every sort of bird and flower. This profusion makes the region seem larger than it is. Dawn comes early to the Thousand Islands then, and the skies hold light till ten at night. On full-moon summer nights, the trees and ferns on our island are pale gold and the stones are silver. The underwater world is strangely lighted at midnight and softer than the air.

Summer brings the long-awaited plums, peaches, nectarines, watermelons, canteloupes, cabbages, tomatoes, onions, beets, carrots, beans, lettuce, and radishes—fresh fruits and vegetables you cannot have at any other time of year except in the form of those taste-less imitations sold in supermarkets. When summer comes we listen and look to discover who will have the first corn. It is usually an Indian family on Tar Island, and as soon as we learn their corn is ripe we go to their farm to pick it ourselves. Nothing is so good as the first picking of the first corn, none so astonishing as that brought to table within an hour of its picking. Often enough our wants are anticipated, and the corn comes to us in a small, leaky outboard motorboat full of tiny Indi-ans. If you ask for a dozen ears, they will give you nine-teen. I have often wondered if someone had told them "nineteen to the dozen." The Indian children, however, think that twelve are not enough because the sweet first new ears are so small.

If summer is warm and fair, full of light, lavish with things good to eat, and if you can dip in the morning, swim most of the afternoon and dip again before bed at night, there is no past and no future. At any season islands keep a different time from mainlands, but on an island in high summer there is only summertime. In this curious time only the children grow older.

We basked pleasantly in summer's opulence, una-ware of the process that was taking place, except to note that as our children became more competent to take care of themselves we became freer to venture from the island by ourselves. Our relationship with the Bodines, the Da-vidsons, and the Rahes changed from one of communal child-watching in the sunlight to include grown-up parties in the evening. The Davidsons brought Montreal to us, and the Rahes the New York theater, and I suppose they were intrigued by the apparent improvidence of our way of life. In any case, we shared a love of the river and the pleasure of one another's company, and meanwhile our children surreptitiously grew older and larger until their changing needs suddenly clamored for attention.

Chris was nearing high-school age, which meant we had to think in terms of a more serious education than that provided by the Maryland county school system. Although we did not know whether our children would wish to enter colleges, we felt we must provide them with the sort of secondary education that would prepare them to do so and one which, in any event, would give them something more valuable to chew on than the Maryland schools did. Moreover, it was time to introduce them to urban civilization. We knew of a competent school in Philadelphia and moved there in order that our children could attend it. The first thing they learned was that walking on pavements gave you shin splints and that ice-cream cones were not five cents, but fifteen cents. They also learned the school would not permit them to leave early in spring and return late in fall. No longer could we be islanders. For a term of years we would have to be summer people.

Christopher's entry in the log reflects the change: "June 7. Nous commençons un beau voyage avec notre ami Nicolai Fessenden, mais, on the Pa. Turnpike we ran into a young buck and notre radiator was gebusten. So we rent de l'auto, and arrivons à six heures après un bon start à quatre heures. Water extremely low, below stavings. Water temp. 59."

The presence of a classmate indicated the beginning of another stage: Our children would grow increasingly apart from us and from each other, meeting new people and bringing them as their guests to the island in summer. For Margaret and me the move to the city was also the beginning of something new. It meant our taking part in school and community affairs, becoming involved in committees trying to solve the problems of urban existence. Writing proceeds from experience, and mine edged away from the hunting and fishing magazines to books which commented on the houses people bought, the way they lived, the automobiles they drove, and the schools their children attended. I would do the research in the city and the writing on the island in summer, and as my work began to embrace themes more complicated than catching fish, it was important for us to bring to the island people who understood these themes and who could discuss them with me and read and criticize the work in progress. In brief, both we and our children began to bring civilization to the island, at some risk of losing the island in the process.

An island can be lost quickly or gradually. It can be invaded and overrun, or infiltrated and subverted by foreign ways and ideas. One of the summer people, old Captain Dash, warned us about this. He was an ancient oak from older river days who had what he called a camp on a wooded island upstream from ours. He was magnificently mustachioed, and with an antique gold-braided yachting skipper's cap pulled down on his white hair, he stood to the wheel amidships in his venerable slow launch when he went out upon the river. He was a man who believed that once you have a thing where you want it, you should make sure it stays there. Each night he dressed in his evening kit to take his supper in the high-ceilinged and pine-paneled dining room of his camp. His manservant brought him cutlets and a split bottle of champagne. One night he told us he had made a mistake in allowing a power line to be brought to his camp.

"Electricity," he said, "takes all the sting out of pioneering."

So can the presence of others. Agents, editors, photographers, a television producer, the classmates of our children, their parents, Philadelphians, Canadians from Ottawa and Montreal, the Bodines and their friends, the summer people we knew, all came to our island in summer. The river meanwhile filled with fishermen, campers, people in cruisers who threw beer cans in the water, and newer and larger tour boats stuffed with tourists. All who came to the island were our friends, and we were always glad to see them, but an entry in the log for one of those summers says, "Three weeks without guests!" It was a cry of relief in Margaret's handwriting, for she took the brunt of it. Each morning I would go to work at the head of the island, guests or no guests, and it was Margaret who had to plan the meals and go to the mainland for the food and worry that the boats' gas tanks were filled and see to our friends and keep an eye on their small children and prepare lunch till I got through my day's work and was able to help. There were times when

it seemed we were operating a combined snack bar, hotel, house party, and summer resort with planned entertainment. The presence of all these people, enjoyable
and necessary as it was, required planning and work that
tended to divorce us from the river and at times made the
island seem not an island but a suburb.

Once a New York editor came to work with me on
a manuscript. We cut and rewrote in the mornings in my
office, talked about the shape of the book in the after-
noons, swam, and after supper returned to literary and
city topics. We might as well have been on Madison
Avenue, taking a dip in his club's pool after work. On the
last day of his stay, however, he wanted to take us all out
to dinner—and this brought us back to the place we
lived.

There are several restaurants and hotels in the river
towns of the Thousand Islands area where you can dine
in bourgeois comfort. The ambiance consists of candles
on the tables, a list of New York State wines, beef Stroga-
noff, a waitress who is working her way through college
and somehow always finds a way to tell you this, canned
fruit in the macedonia, and a stiff price. We told the
editor we would be delighted to dine out, but because of
the distance we would have to go we should plan to leave
the island at six in the evening. No, we told him and two
Philadelphia house guests, we would not have to dress,
but we should take rain gear in the boat.

We went downriver in a luminous late-afternoon
light beneath a Maxfield Parrish sky. Work and the city
dissolved in the warmth and distances of high summer as
we motored slowly along the flanks of Grenadier Island

and close inshore to enjoy the shapes of cliffs and coves; as we swung out to take our friends past those desolate offshore islands that were our favorite picnic grounds and then inside shoal water to the marshes, past Minnie Buell's farm where we would go for butter, out past the old lighthouse on Three Sisters Island. We were bound for the foot of Grenadier. It was a lonely part of the river, full of shoals. There were no houses visible, save the steep-roofed brooding pile of the castle on Dark Island far downstream. The American shoreline was a green smudge on the horizon, lying beneath the rose and white gold towers of a gigantic thunderhead. We could not hear the thunder, but we could see the cumulo-nimbus light up like a Chinese lantern; see the light billow through the piled-high rolling mass, then flicker along the banner of ice crystals that was wind-driven into the east.

You keep along shelving rock as you enter the cove at the very foot of Grenadier. At the far end of the cove are a cat-o'-nine-tails marsh and an unpainted wooden dock. Beyond that and set beneath great trees are a bit of lawn and a small white house. The house was (and is) a restaurant, advertised nowhere, approachable only by boat, and dangerous to approach if you do not know the way through the shoals. We wanted to dine early in order to be able to see our way down and back while there was light. The reason for our coming to Heffernan's, as the restaurant was called, was the beauty of that rather wild and deserted part of the river. The patrons of this establishment were fishing guides and the parties they brought there, and they came for the food.

So far as I know, the menu has never changed. It consists of a green salad with a dressing of oil, salt, vinegar, and paprika; pickles and cheese; potatoes, beets, and corn; fried chicken; hot rolls; a choice of apple, cherry, or blueberry pie with or without ice cream; coffee, tea, or milk. You can send the bowls and platters back as often as you please. You can have four pieces of each kind of pie if you wish (I remember that one of my son's friends did). It is a meal of plain, homely fare for hungry fishermen. All the food comes from the farm adjoining the restaurant and is cooked in the kitchen. When we went there with the editor the price was three dollars a person. As far as we are concerned, it is the only place in the area to dine out. Nowhere else do you have the same view of marsh, trees, stone, sky, and water. Past a screen of oaks, and far out on that wide water, you can see the neat, classical lines of the abandoned lighthouse and steamships nudging up against the current in the Seaway.

The thunderheads gathered while we were eating, and Maxfield Parrish stopped painting them. The sky turned black. There was a sudden wind and a cannonade. A lightning flash showed *Margaret* rising and falling at dockside, shining wetly in the rain. Instead of leaving as quickly as it came, the storm worsened. We had more coffee. At eleven that night the decision was to go home in the storm. We simply could not spend the night there, particularly because there were children on the island.

The five of us, bundled into ponchos and coats that could not keep out all the rain that bucketed gustily down upon us, set warily out in the smother. My eyeglasses were at once rain-smeared, and I had to use a finger as a windshield wiper. We steered out of the cove by lightning flashes that at once blinded us and let us know where we were. We could not go back the way we had come, because that water was too full of rocks to be risked in the sporadic illumination provided by the lightning. We would follow instead the winking buoys of the American ship channel.

While our drenched house guests sat huddled in the stern, the editor soaking in the port bucket seat, Margaret sat next to me on the engine box to help find the way. Where do you think we are? I would ask, and she, who did not wear glasses, would mutter her opinions. We kept our voices down because we felt it would not do to create among our guests the impression that we were quite as lost as they. We were meanwhile plowing into a storm-driven head sea that sent sheets of water glittering over the boat, lighted by our red and green bow lights as they hurtled past. We found the channel's blinking lights. We timed their flashes, recognized their order, and learned where we were.

"What's that light behind us?" one of our house guests called, her voice rather dubious and somewhat shrill.

The light was not only behind us but above us. It was a great green glare towering overhead and just astern, and lurid beneath it was an enormous white breaking wave.

"Turn! Get out of the way! We're right under their bow! They can't see us!" Margaret said urgently into my ear.

I opened the *Margaret*'s throttle, hauled on the tiller, and broke sharply to starboard. The vast bulk of the steamship loomed out of the storm, sliding into the water we had just fled, and as we turned we could now see the bright gaiety of her stern cabin lights following along behind her. These lights also showed the red buoy off the foot of Three Sisters Island, and they showed that we were on the wrong side of that buoy. In fact, we were on course for the shoal it marked. I cut the engine, hoped for the best, and, answering our house guest's question, said, "That's a steamship. She looks like an ore boat."

We seemed to have glided safely over that shoal, or possibly safely through its tumbled stones. I started the *Margaret* again and this time followed the stern lights of the ship that had nearly run us down until we could see Grenadier Island's winking light off the starboard beam. Now the only obstacle between us and our island was the Whisky Island shoal. A lightning bolt illuminated it for us. There it was, a dozen yards off the port bow. We arrived home at midnight, soaked and thankful. We thanked the editor for the good dinner he had given us, and he and our Philadelphia friends thanked us and their lucky stars for the lovely boat ride we had. Since they were wet, tired, and had to leave next morning, they went straight away to bed while Margaret and I, still excited by the danger we had run and of which our friends had not been entirely aware, changed into dry clothing and went out on the porch to have a nightcap.

The storm left us. The air was suddenly warm and still, and we enjoyed the play of lightning moving far downriver. We heard a boat arrive and voices call, "Are you still up?"

In the boat were friends from Ottawa whom we had not seen for three years. They had been coming down-river to see us that night, they said, but there had been a storm and they had taken shelter from it at a friend's place, and they knew it was late but they did want to see us and would only stay a minute. Would we like a night-cap? They had brought a bottle.

Two hours later, when they went to start their out-board motor, the starting cord pulled right out of it. We suggested they stay the night; we could make beds for them on the porch gliders; we would worry about their boat in the morning.

But no, it seemed they had children asleep in the motel they were stopping in upriver; they knew it was all very dreadful, but could we give them a tow? They were staying just up past the bridge. Margaret felt she should stay behind so that there would be one of us on the island while we had guests there, and I went upriver with our Ottawa friends in tow.

Now, "just up past the bridge" is that island maze that so astonished first the Indians and now the tourists with its compelling beauty. While I am reasonably sure of my way around in it, I had just a bit of difficulty that night. For fog closed in as we entered the maze. It was not till five in the morning that I felt my way back to the island where Margaret still waited on the porch, a candle burning. The candle winked out as I landed, and Margaret was climbing into bed when I came up the boathouse stairs.

"We better get some sleep," she said, "because our guests have to be up at seven."

Another family was to arrive the following day, but they came that afternoon instead.

"I know we're a day early," the wife explained, "but it was so hot and awful in town and we kept thinking how cool and wonderful and peaceful it is here that we just couldn't wait to come."

10

In the extraordinary length of a fair summer's identical days and in the invitation of her lovely nights, we
could not feel pressed by time even if there were fourteen around the long oak table. Such was the strange
quality of summer's ephemeral infinity that our season
on the river seemed larger and of greater duration than
all the rest of the year. The island was where we lived.
The city was where we went to camp for the winter.

There were not always guests on the island, and
then we had it to ourselves, together with its birds and
animals. The animals, it seemed, had come across from
the mainland on the winter ice and were marooned when
the ice went out in spring. The family of snowshoe rab-

bits who ate Victoria's petunias had wintered over, as had the red and black squirrels. You could almost tell time by one red squirrel. Perhaps in another life he had been a railway man or a banker; maybe a watchman. At seven-fifteen he pattered across the boathouse roof, jumped to the staircase railing, and ran off to his appointments. At eleven-thirty I would see him jump from one pine bough to a neighboring tree outside my windows at the head of the island, and in the afternoon at three-twenty-five he would be in the black oak by the playhouse. One year, tracing a leak in the bunkhouse, we came upon a squirrel's nest built between the bunkhouse's double walls, and in that nest was a round porcelain saltcellar. We had wondered what had happened to it, and now we wondered how the squirrel had managed to carry it from the kitchen shelf out to the bunkhouse and into the nest. Obviously, he was a squirrel who liked salted nuts.

We were always eager to know what animals were in residence when we arrived, but sometimes weeks passed before we found out. We heard the raccoon for days before we got a glimpse of him. Once we thought there was a fox. If so, he must have subsisted chiefly on the island's permanent population of voles. A less welcome visitor was a large Norway rat that may have deserted a Seaway steamship. We heard him chewing and at last saw him nibbling his way into the kitchen. A trap was set, and next day the children tied a burned-out generator coil around the rat's dead neck, together with a card to Davy Jones, and returned him to the river. The animal that provoked the most excitement was one we first saw as a flickering shadow moving at speed over a gray boulder. Some mornings later we saw it again—a slender shape disappearing into a woodpecker's hole in a dead tree. I was sure it was a weasel, and Margaret wanted to get rid of it to protect the island's birds. We watched it emerge from the tree and bound through the summer grass to disappear into our woodpile. There was a strong musky scent there, somewhat like a skunk's.

All that morning Christopher sat like a stone on a grassy slope, a .22-caliber air rifle in his hands. I worked at the head of the island, Margaret was busy in the kitchen, and the girls played in and out of the house while the boy sat dead still, waiting. The animal showed its head, Chris took aim, and Victoria burst out of the kitchen door, slamming it open. Stop that, Chris told her. But the animal had vanished. An hour later it ventured tentatively out from between the logs, and the boy fired.

Margaret came to tell me to stop work to see what Christopher had shot. It was a beautiful, long, slender, dark-brown thing of rich fur, lying on a log as if asleep. There was a fleck of blood; the boy had shot it through the eye. We all thought it was a weasel, but the weasels we knew had little black masks, reddish coats, and wonderfully white vests.

"Let's ask Dr. Creighton what it is," Chris suggested, and time stood still while we went downriver.

Professor William S. Creighton and his wife, Martha, lived in the house they had built on Huckleberry Point at the foot of Tar Island. Dr. Creighton was the world's foremost authority on the taxonomy of the ants of North America. In his other guises, Bill was a biologist, a dead shot with pistol and rifle, a Virginia gentleman, hunter, fisherman, carpenter, plumber, mechanic, electrician, gardener, stonemason, collector of risqué verse, parodist, and judge of good whisky. In all these attributes and accomplishments, with the exception of Virginia descent and expertise in small arms and electronics, Marty was his helpmeet. When Chris and I arrived with our dead animal, Marty was helping Bill lever a huge stone, weighing several hundred pounds, out of its bed, to be skidded on rollers to a seawall they were building. They were both dressed in stone-dusty shirts and trousers, sweating like field hands.

"I swear, JK, that damned *Miss Brockville* is the curse of the river," Bill said as we landed. "But when I get this wall finished, she can throw all the wake she wants and the hell with her. Here, give me your line."

"Look, if you're working we'll come back later," I said.

"Oh, come in and sit," Marty said. "It's time we had a break. Where did you get that mink?"

"Is that what it is? We were going to ask you. Chris shot it."

"Well, good for you," Bill told Chris. "Yes, it's a mink. It's a female and she has kits. She's lactating."

He showed us the wet on the belly fur.

"Right in the eye," Bill said. "Good for you, Chris."

"Did you find the kits?" Marty wanted to know.

When we explained the circumstances, the Creightons guessed the baby minks would be found in a nest in the woodpile. While Marty stroked the soft fur and told us that minks could swim and fish, Bill went into their house for a scalpel, scissors, and arsenic. He showed us how to skin the animal, scrape the hide, peg it out to dry, and dust the fur with arsenic to keep insects out of it. The peeled animal was a beautiful thing. You could see the bands of muscles; how perfectly it was designed for speed and murder. We moved its legs and back to see how the muscles slid, admired it, and threw it into the reeds for the turtles and the fish. Marty brought out bottles of ale. We chatted for a while and returned upriver with the mink pelt pegged out on a board to dry in the sun, while Bill and Marty went back to their crow-bars and their enormous stone.

We took the woodpile apart carefully, as if we were playing jackstraws. There were five kittens in the nest. One had its teeth, and I had a bitten thumb before we had them in a box filled with wood shavings and bound around with screening wire. Margaret and the girls went to the mainland to call Ralph Peck to say we had shot a mink out of season, and the game warden arrived to collect the babies and send them on to the Toronto zoo. The dressed pelt hangs today on the living-room wall, and whenever we see it we remember the shadow sliding over the stone and what happened after that.

The pelt on the wall belongs to The Summer We Shot the Mink, but we cannot remember what summer that was without looking in the log, for all those summers merged together into one long summertime when we would wind up the Victrola in the early morning and wait for Caruso to wake the guests; when there were swimming parties and drinks on summer people's docks;

when we all learned to water ski, held underwater treasure hunts, and lived on and in the water. The water skiing soon bored us. Unlike real skiing, there is not the same quality of danger, feel of speed, or demand for thought. Bubbling around on the bottom of the river in an Aqualung, looking for hidden bottles containing clues to the location of the next bottle, was much more fun— at least for me. The *Nomad* belonged to those summers, and to more summers than we knew.

She was a fifty-foot cruiser, an antique of sedate pace, a comfortable old shoe with beer in her false funnel, the custodian of a gentle history. Her crew in summers past had been young Montreal boys dressed in singlets lettered *Nomad.* In addition to cruising the Rideau, Ottawa, and St. Lawrence rivers, the boys looked forward to going foreign. They would sail her down to United States waters to a favorite anchorage in a little cove of Lake Champlain. One summer after the First World War, *Nomad* anchored there, and old boys from the crew went ashore to fix to granite a bronze plaque bearing the names of *Nomad*'s war dead. After the Second World War, *Nomad* paid another visit to that cove. It is a simple monument, the only one to foreign warriors on United States soil: a bit of bronze, a few names, and a memory of children in summertime.

She came to call at Fancy Rock one summer day, and Gordon Davidson, who once upon a time had been one of those boys in singlets, introduced us to her owners. We became friends, and Chris was invited to join the crew.

Nomad sailed into our summer just in time to give Chris an understanding of the value of summers he had never known, before it was time for him to leave the river. His cruises on *Nomad* marked the end of one phase of life for him and the beginning of something else. In the summer between his junior and senior years in high school he was one of six students chosen to attend a work camp abroad. He sailed for France and England and in the process left the island, the river, and his childhood behind him. The following summer he worked in the city to help pay his way in college and in the college summers after that. We were sorry to lose him and glad to see him go.

With her brother grown away, the full light of summer fell upon our daughter Margaret, and the island bloomed with pretty girls. When seven of her Philadelphia classmates came together to visit us, I discovered what it must be like to preside over a harem. For one thing, the quantity of lemons consumed is enormous. Fifteen-year-old girls do not eat them; juice of lemon is the essence of whatever brew they concoct in which to wash their hair. Next, they leave things everywhere. Finally, if your harem consists of nubile maidens, all you are likely to get to eat are chocolate chip cookies. You are also likely to be the only one eating them, because it will appear the girls are all on diets. One of our daughter's friends was a delightful exception to this rule. When the others were all talking of ways and means to preserve their girlish figures, this one ran her hands along her hips, surveyed herself with quiet pride, and shrugged her pleasant architecture.

"Oh, I don't know," she said. "I'm glad I have some meat on me."

A silent majority compressed its lips into little lines, slaughter in its eyes.

However much may be said to the contrary, I believe that women see and think differently from men and that this difference is complementary, necessary, and invaluable. If I look at a tree, my first concern is to note its shape, bark, and leaves in order to classify it. A woman may certainly do this, too, but she is first likely to see the birds in its branches. "Oh, look at the song sparrow," she will say, and I, following her glance, will ask, "In the white oak?" I learned, or think I learned, something about girls when they came to our island, if only not to inquire too closely into their mysteries.

"What are they doing?" I asked my wife one morning, seeing them all on the swimming dock surrounded by bottles of lotions.

"Chris and Jon Fox are coming today," she explained.

"Yes, but they won't be in till late afternoon. It is now eight o'clock."

My wife regarded me pityingly.

When the student princes arrived at last, they paid no attention to the demure nubility.

"You all know everyone, don't you?" my wife asked, looking from the boys to the girls. Of course they did; the school they attended was small.

"Yeah," Chris said. "Hi."

"Yeah. Hi," Jon said.

With that, the boys went to stow their dunnage, the girls silently watching them climb the stairs.

When the boys returned to swim away the fatigue of the drive from Philadelphia, it appeared that the girl who was not worried about her weight had another worry instead. She had a fishing line, a hook, and a worm. For a week she and the other girls had pulled in panfish with competent delight, cold-bloodedly cutting up the worms, baiting the hooks, killing and cleaning the fish, their hands grubby with blood, dirt, scales, and slime. Now, however, the meatier girl (as she might not at that moment have described herself) had completely forgotten how to do any of this.

"Ooof! He's wiggling!" she said, making a face as she sought, ineptly, to put the worm on her hook.

"Well, hold him tight," Chris explained.

"Oh, I can't," she said, looking at Jon.

"Here, I'll show you how," Jon said. "Let me have him."

The helpless girl remained, however, where she stood, and Jon had to go to her. She held the hook and worm in such a way that Jon had to reach around her pretty waist to help her with her problem. It next developed that when she caught a perch she had no idea how to get it off the hook, but by this time she had Jon's entire attention—as well as that of all the other girls.

When, however, the boys took their disturbing presence back to the city, the eight young women returned to being fifteen years old again and regained a camaraderie that had been briefly jangled. One evening after supper we went out on the night water to serenade island people we knew. The girls' clear young voices carried well in the still evening. Our friends came to stand at water's edge among the fireflies, silent, listening. They saw the *Margaret*'s dark shape and burning running lights, while from the starlit river water maidens' voices rose and softly fell through the lovely cadences of "Greensleeves."

"More!" the people ashore would call when they found voices of their own. "Please! Won't you come ashore?"

But not until we reached the foot of Tar Island did we go ashore. The Creightons stood on the stones of Huckleberry Point listening to the girls' songs. They loved to sing, themselves, and wanted us all to come sing with them in their house. Bill said he would tune up his ancient banjo. Equally to the point, Marty called, "And let's all eat watermelon!"

The girls were enchanted by the Creightons. I suppose that age fifteen is vulnerable to dreams and that one enduring dream of boy or girl growing up in America is to go off into the wilderness with your love to build a house with your own hands and surround it with your garden. Since this was in fact what the Creightons had done, they may have seemed to represent that dream come true.

Thinking of girls in summer, I could see, perhaps for the first time, the woman in our child. One of the fascinating things about girls, or women, is their age. This has nothing to do with chronology. Nothing can be more distracting than the calm, understanding glance of a five-year-old woman, who, regarding you with the eyes of the Cumean Sibyl, recognizes you for exactly what you are—interesting, necessary, but merely a man—no matter what the world may think of you. Girls move instantaneously and unthinkingly in and out of childhood and womanhood from moment to moment. Despite glimpses of her womanhood as she grows, when you live with your daughter from day to day you are not truly aware of an ongoing process, and you continue to think of her as a child. It is different with a son. Having spent some time as a boy myself, I felt I knew what my son was all about, and I could see him stumbling through all the familiar stages. Never having been a girl, I had no way of imagining what that was. Of course I should have suspected that if there is a man in a boy, there just as plainly would be a woman in a girl, but it was only after seeing other girls on the island that I began to see the woman emergent in our daughter. She was dainty, petite, and precise if not fastidious. Although perfectly competent at running the boats, she did not take quite the same pleasure in it that her mother did. Always content to let someone else take charge, she expected that boys or men would. Perhaps in growing up with us, and in her experience of rural Canada and its school, she had got it firmly fixed in her head that men and women have specifically different roles to play and that the show's success is absolutely dependent on how well each member of the cast performs. I suspect, however, that she largely came this way and that acculturation had very little to do with her femininity. I remember her once stepping off a Maryland school bus when she was very small and the bus seeming to tilt as all the boys crowded in its windows to shout goodbye.

"Why didn't you answer them?" I asked.

"They like it better if I don't," she said.

While young Margaret was far more interested in fashion and the domestic arts than her mother was, and much as she may have preferred to bake while men and boys split wood, she was sufficiently loyal to us, and understanding of the needs of the island, to help with whatever work was going on. Moreover, she was good at it. Her brother and Bocy went at things slapdash when they were her age, stepping in the paint can in the course of painting the dock and then jumping in the *Margaret* to track paint onto her varnished rail and seat cushions, but Margaret painted docks and walls with a cabinetmaker's infinite care.

At just the time my wife and I were basking in the comfort of a helpful daughter, away she went into a summertime of her own. As with Chris, we were sorry to lose her and glad to see her go. As far as we were concerned, it made much more sense for her to work elsewhere in summer than to hang around the river. We never thought much of those teenagers who did hang around, except to feel a pity that they could not find something more constructive to do than racket around all night in speeding boats. In the summer of her junior year in high school, Margaret took a job as an *au pair* girl with a family on the Atlantic coast. The summer after that, she was the lowliest clerk in a Philadelphia publishing house—saving money to look for work in London. It seemed that all the girls in the world wanted to live in London then, just as once upon a time they had all wanted to live in New York.

We were left with one chick cheeping somewhat loudly in the nest. The following lustrum of our summertime would be entirely Victoria's—insofar as parental attention was concerned. Our attention, however, had never been wholly parental. The children lived with us on the island—not the other way around. They shared our attention with work, the people of Rockport, summer people, guests, fishing, swimming, and the weather. If you are lucky, having children is a process of having less and less to do with them, and I am sure that the children would have it so. While ours were growing up and beginning to leave, I am certain that they shared in our lives and our pleasures. But I am equally certain that the center of our lives was fixed on the island, whereas theirs was not, nor should it have been so. Their need was to venture into the world to find islands of their own. We had found ours.

"Which is your island?" a guest once asked as we brought her and her husband across the river from the mainland. She was seeing the region for the first time.

It was sunset, and shafts of light, piercing high clouds, touched the river here and there. One of them fell full upon our island while other islands remained in shadow.

"Ours," my wife said, "is the house with the golden windows."

II

Late one summer afternoon I found Will standing
alone on the Bodines' lawn, looking appraisingly at the
cottage that had once belonged to old Mr. Weeks. I
asked him what he had in mind for it now, for it was Will
who had enlarged the original small farmhouse, built its
chimney of stones gathered from different islands,
paneled its walls, added the porch, a front bedroom on
the second story, and the stone steps.

"Oh, nothing," he said. "I was just looking. Gee,
there's a lot of my life in that house."

There was indeed, and more of Will's life in the
grounds as well. Will had tended the lawn, the fruit trees,
and had built the boathouse, the shops, the docks, and

the house at the lower end of the property where he and Effie lived. There was even more of Will's life in the lives of others, or in their memories. They remembered him as a young man, diving over the bow of an ore ship several hundred feet long, to bob up grinning astern. Some people had bet he wouldn't do it, and Will told them, "If you put up five dollars I won't, I'll put up a dollar that says I will."

"What them fellows forgot," Will told me, "was that the ship wouldn't stop. She had too much weight on her to stop even if she wanted to. There was nothing to it. All you do is jump over, go deep and hold your breath, and she'll go right over you. Anybody can hold his breath that long."

There was also the time when old Mr. Weeks and his male guests had wanted Will to take them fishing early one morning, and it was Will who thought of a way to rouse them without waking their women and children. He would keep the alarm clock down to his house, he said, and when it woke him, he'd come up alongside the cottage at five in the morning and give a little tug on the fishing line that would be tied to the big toe of the fellow sleeping in the side bedroom. Early that next morning, Will gave a little tug, but there was no response. So Will put the fish line over his shoulder and started running, and my, he said, did that fellow ever holler! His foot came right out the open window, with him bellowing, and that started the women shouting and the kids crying, and all the men laughing fit to die. They caught some dandy fish that day, too.

It was not long after that late afternoon, when Will

stood as straight-backed as ever, a slight, still strong old man looking at the Bodine house and seeing his life, that he told me he was going to paint the cottage next year, "if I live." I suppose he knew he would not.

I cannot say that we mourn Will's death, because we still see him everywhere. He is in the stern sheets of the old scarlet outboard, telling Margaret he had a dandy fish tied up for her in the next cove, that he'd swing the boat to drag the bait right by him for her, and then, by gee, Margaret had a whale. And there is Will, grinning like an ape, saying, "Well, that's the funniest-looking fish I ever did see!" as the waterlogged cabbage came up along side.

You cannot go past the shelving rock at the foot of Will's bay and not see him squatting there in his old felt hat, shirt, and work trousers, showing a small boy how to clean a fish. He is on the sun-baked unpainted boards of the dock, putting shellac on a child's cut, and then painting all the children's feet with it "so the gravel won't hurt." When you go onto his porch, you find him rocking with your small daughter on his knees, singing, "The silliest thing I ever saw/Was sipping cider through a straw . . ." If you look out across the river and think it unusually high this year, Will will tell you why this is.

"You know how when you fill a pail right up with water, and then you drop a bass in it, how some water will slop out of her? Well, it's the same with the lakes up west. When them flounders multiply, why, they lay on the bottom of the lakes one on top of each other three and four foot high, and it's just like you put a bass in a bucket.

Some of the water has got to spill out, and of course it spills out of the lakes and comes down the river.

"It's a funny thing about them fish spawning," the old man will say. "You see some funny things on the river. If you ever see a big bunch of eels come down the river, all tangled up in a big squirmy ball, if you was to hit them eels with an oar, you'll see a big blacksnake come shooting right out of the middle of that ball. That snake was in there all the time, and it was him that was making them spawn."

When you go inside Will's house today, you will find him and Effie sitting in the living room, listening to *The Romance of Helen Trent* on the radio, arguing with each other whether the ingenue can really be so foolish not to know what that young villain meant to do. "Why, I wouldn't trust a fellow like that for anything," Effie will tell you.

She was not long in following Will. We arrived at their house one summer day to learn that two of her friends had, moments earlier, entered the living room to find her on the floor. They had got her to a couch. No, they had not called an ambulance, but if we said to, they would be glad to do it. They thought they should call the ambulance, they said, but the ambulance would be fifteen dollars. It was good we had come, they said, because we could take the responsibility.

Like Will, we see Effie everywhere, and she is always making fried cakes in the kitchen with children about her. "There now," Effie tells them, "everybody take two, one for each hand."

Will and Effie died at some time during the enormous summer of our lives on the island, but it is at once difficult and unimportant to say just when. They are still a part of the river and the islands, just as Rockport is the same now as it was before they built the Bridge, except of course it is different. After they built the Bridge they gave up the ferry, and Cornwall's store is now Terry's, and Hickory Lodge was burned down and where it was is a public campsite, but nothing has changed because the old store and summer hotel are still there in the same way that Will and Effie are still bailing with a bucket and Will's felt hat when the stick went through the hull of their boat.

Perhaps you do not mourn the deaths of people, places, and things, and the deaths of times and ways, if you live on a river. Continually moving, the river remains within its same banks, apparently as wide and as deep as ever, rising and falling as always in its seasons, neither starting nor stopping, but always in motion and changing while seeming to remain exactly the same.

Precise moments can be vividly recalled. We can still hear the smashing, clattering, clanking of the *Margaret*'s crankshaft breaking, and we can remember the summer when the *Margaret* sat high and dry on timbers in the boathouse because there was no money to buy a new engine, but we cannot recall what summer that was because it seems a moment ago and because we still think of the *Margaret*'s engine as the new one. In point of fact (I have now looked it up in the log), the new engine is eleven years old, and Ed Huck fitted it into the boat the year after Will died. It now seems to me, in a retrospect that cannot be measured on any calendar, that many changes began to affect the changeless river in those years. Changes were taking place in America, and America began to come to the river. As a new high-speed multilane divided highway began to stretch from Philadelphia toward the Thousand Islands Bridge, many new cottages grew along the Canadian shoreline between the Bodines' cottage and Rockport. Others appeared on islands where in prior years we had gone to gather berries and to swim. New kinds of boats with new kinds of engines, driven by a very different sort of boatman, began to move more thickly and swiftly on the river in summer.

The new boats were made of fiberglass, a material possessing many advantages over wood. They could be made rapidly and cheaply in molds. There was no need to paint, for the colors were mixed into the plastic. There were no seams to caulk; the boats did not have to be put into the river to soak, or take up, as the people said, before they could be used. The hulls did not rot. Maintenance was simplicity itself. At the end of a season, you pulled the boat out of water, wiped it off with a damp rag, and that was that. To ready it for the next season, you wiped off the winter's dust and put it in the water. The smallest of these new plastic boats were powered by outboard motors that each year increased in horsepower, until eventually they began to resemble shiny little plastic ironing boards with a hundred horsepower astern. The largest were cabin cruisers with flying bridges above their bridges, plastic carpets wall to wall, color television, and picture windows.

Boats, we felt, should be made of wood. They should be slowly and carefully built by craftsmen who had respect for themselves and a respect for what they were doing. They should be used by people who had respect for the craftsmen and for the long traditions of the sea. There are many psychological reasons why boats and ships are considered female, all of them having to do with love and caring. It was difficult for us to imagine a plastic boat as "she"; much easier to think of it as "it."

One result of the new age was that, almost at once, the need for boatwrights dramatically diminished. Old Ed Andress was virtually alone in building wooden boats with the tools of the Bronze Age and the skills of all the centuries since then. The proprietors of riverside marinas became salesmen rather than artisans, and they employed mechanics instead of ship carpenters.

The faster the plastic craft multiplied, the more they began to resemble automobiles. They came festooned with rear-view mirrors, radio antennae, wrap-around windscreens that distorted one's vision, automobile-like seats made of imitation leather, automobile-like carpeting on their floorboards, unnecessary and inutile headlights, dials all over their instrument panels. Other non-optional features included the electrically operated overpowered engines, excessive fuel consumption, inflated prices, and garish colors. Wholly apart from their vulgarity, these apparitions seemed to have been designed by salesmen rather than by seamen. They were built for speeding over placid lakes in a dead calm, for their freeboard was often low enough to guarantee a drenching for anyone sitting anywhere in them in a cross wind, and their hulls bounced and pounded on the slightest ripple. The hydraulic springs beneath their seats were a clue to the kind of ride to expect. We wondered why, if a boat is to be made of molded plastic, it could not at least be shaped like a boat—molded to a sea-kindly design. Evidently this could be done, for there were beautifully shaped sailboats made of fiberglass. We could only think that the people who bought the tarted-up, unseaworthy and overpowered craft must have had no experience on water. And this, it seemed, was often the case.

"Where am I?" one of the new boatmen called to us as we sat on the swimming dock one summer day. "Which way is Alexandria Bay?"

We asked if he had a chart.

"I never use one of those things," he said. "I've seen a chart. I've seen a lot of charts. All they show is a lot of water."

We told him where he was and pointed toward the shoal-strewn way to Alexandria Bay. Away he roared in his plastic water car, bouncing, splashing, and pounding at forty miles an hour toward whatever destination awaited him.

"He could have said 'Thanks,'" someone said.

"No, he couldn't," Gordon Davidson observed.

The new boatmen were smashing around the river at speed without the faintest idea of the International Rules of the Road, nor any clue to what the horn signals were—much less what they meant. As the new boats and the new boatmen appeared, the accidents began. A quality of danger was added to our summer. On weekends in high summer there began to be so many boats darting about in the Canadian channel that we remained on the island, not only to keep out of the way of people who did not know what they were doing but also to keep clear of the noise they made. This was not always a complete defense, for one summer day while we were reading in the living room there was a sound like someone slamming a manhole lid on a steel boiler, simultaneous with an explosion in a china factory.

Thinking our pantry shelves must have given way, breaking every glass and dish we owned, Margaret and I went to inspect the damage. The shelves were all in place, the glasses and dishes sitting serenely on them. We heard voices, and going out on the dining porch and looking over the side, we saw a houseboat roosting in our birch trees. We had heard its steel hull slamming up on the shelving rock of our island and all of its dishes breaking.

"The chart shows there's four feet of water off this island," the houseboat's skipper angrily called up to us.

"That may be true," I told him, "but you're not in the water, you're on the island."

I could not understand how anyone at high noon on a bright day could have come a mile across open water to collide at full speed with an island, nor did the shipwrecked sailors offer any explanation. They seemed to feel that we had hurled our island under their boat, and what were we going to do about that?

Using the *Margaret,* we towed them off the rock. They came from Pennsylvania, they told us, and none of them had ever been in any sort of boat before that very morning. The woman was now afraid they might have put a hole in the steel hull and wondered what to do.

"Take it back and tell them it doesn't work," I suggested, disgusted with the whole affair and particularly with the kind of man who would put two tons of unwieldy houseboat into the hands of such navigators.

The numbers of rented houseboats grew, too. They became so plentiful that Gordon took to calling them St. Lawrence Sampans. They were typically rented to well-meaning young families who were genuinely sorry if, in the course of their inexpert landing at a village dock, they whacked into someone's varnished mahogany launch.

"Until them houseboats showed up," one riverman told us, "the worst thing we had on the river was fog."

I disagreed. I felt the new cruisers were the worst of the lot. They too began to arrive on the river in increasing numbers, huge plastic affairs typically flying flags showing wineglasses to indicate the people aboard were drinkers. Inside they carried little plaques reading, "Any marriages performed by the captain of this vessel are valid only for the duration of the voyage." Typically, too, their owners' qualifications as yachtsmen consisted solely of their ability to borrow the down payment. We were fascinated to learn that some of the new cruisers never cruised. They lay moored in vast plastic sheds in Alexandria Bay all summer long, with the people living aboard them as if in motel rooms which, in fact, the cruisers' interiors greatly resembled. These presented no problem; it was the cruisers that bolted about the river that were the dangerous nuisances, and there was one fellow who was particularly impressive.

He wore a hat with gold braid and a blue blazer with gold buttons and a captain's gold braid on its cuffs, ice-cream trousers, and mirror sunglasses. Standing on the flying bridge of his cruiser as he brought her into the Rockport Customs Dock one day, racing to overtake another cruiser that was landing there and imagining that he had been unfairly preceded, this braided mariner was enraged. Seizing his loud-hailer, he boomed, "You son of a bitch, I'll rock you out of the water!" With that, he spun his immense craft around and came roaring flat out beside the dock, spewing a gigantic wake against all the boats moored there, including the one he felt had cheated him. The people who raced out on the dock to save their boats from being banged against it could hear the fellow muttering to himself as he ran away. He had left his loud-hailer on, and his muttered curses echoed over Rockport. They had to do with his decision never to go through Canadian customs again, and with what the Canadians could do with themselves and their country.

That cruiser skipper represented an extreme case of a general swinishness that eventually made going to Heffernan's for supper quite impossible for us. The new cruiser people discovered Heffernan's, and thither they went at the end of a day of drinking and pounding around the river. We can still enjoy an evening there in spring or fall but not in high summer, when the little restaurant fills with the braying of whisky laughter and paunchy jollity of plastic people.

At about the time the cruisers arrived, my writing began to wonder about credit cards and Green Stamps and about the quality of opulent tawdriness that seemed somehow suddenly to have pervaded American life and was now invading what had been a quiet, remote, and timeless corner of the world. One editor characterized me as a counter-puncher, and another likened my writing to a banzai charge. They were commenting on writing done as the plastic age came to the river.

As the houses began to multiply along the riverbanks and on other islands and the boats multiplied on the water, weeds began to appear where none had been before. They grew so thickly that casting and trolling was impossible in many favorite fishing grounds. Their growth was attributed to an increase in untreated sewage from boats, cruisers, houses, and river towns and to a simultaneous increase in the amount of detergents entering the river. The weeds came slowly at first, then more rapidly, and at last explosively. The way around the head of Club Island, a path from our island to the Canadian mainland that offers the best protection from heavy southwest winds, was closed by weeds. Meanwhile the river became less potable. In summers past we had always been able to dip a cup over the side whenever we were thirsty, but no longer. We have always had our water tested by the government laboratories in Toronto, and now the tests showed the presence of fecal bioforms.

A more sinister form of pollution meanwhile appeared. Geordie Heffernan, returning to his island restaurant one night after having ferried the young waitresses to the mainland, found that someone had clubbed his wife unconscious, thrown her into the marsh, and looted the cash register. Thieves stole a boat in Alexandria Bay, stripped it of its electronic equipment, and opened its seacocks to sink it and so destroy evidence of their crime.

The improving highways were bringing all sorts of people to the region, and Alexandria Bay's waterfront reflected this. A shopping center, central to nothing, was opened inland from the Bay. Two waterfront grocery stores went out of business; a drugstore went under; the bank moved away from the river to the new commercial complex; and the once pleasant waterfront filled up with pizza stands, bars with go-go girls wriggling in their windows and signs reading "I.D. Cards Must Be Shown" and "No Bare Feet."

Someone built a house on our favorite picnic island, where the eagles' nest had been. This was the last of the deserted picnic islands to be thus improved, and now no more picnic places remained for us unless we should choose to go to one of the Provincial parks whose docks were full of cruisers.

There was, however, a large empty island near our own that we and the children used to explore. Someone set it afire. We never learned who did, but we heard that people had been camping at the foot of the island before the fire began. No one recognized their boat, an outboard like a thousand others. No doubt they had had a good time camping there and were sure they had extin-

guished their cooking fire before they left. They must
certainly have been strangers to the islands, because
river people know that you cannot safely build a fire on
a carpet of pine needles on a rocky island. The fire will
get into the frost cracks of island stones and will smolder
for days beneath the forest floor before erupting elsewhere.

I have said that my writing changed to reflect an
unease, but the island and the river were by no means
spoiled and lost to us merely because some of the less
enchanting aspects of mankind began to appear in the
region. My wife's mother gave up on the river and never
returned after the first outboard motorboats appeared
years ago, claiming she couldn't stand the noise they
made. She moved to a silent Vermont hilltop to live
alone in a little house we called Widow's Pique, but I
could never really believe that outboard motorboats
should have made all that difference to her, and so far as
the new plastic boats were concerned, I did not like
them, but I did not have to buy one.

In the meantime, the changes meant nothing at all
to Victoria; she loved the island summer quite as much
as we, but for different reasons. Two of them were found
on Fancy Rock: the younger Rahe boys, Christopher and
Roderic Jr. These three had played together every summer of their lives, and if as they grew older the Rahe boys
began to understand that she was a girl, this made no
difference in their acceptance of her. They swam and
water skied and ran around in boats together and took
themselves off to the Thousand Islands Club to learn
tennis from Joe the Pro and to Alexandria Bay for hoag-

ies. Victoria never shared our enthusiasm for fishing, nor was this a principal activity of her friends. To her, summer meant sunshine and water, tennis and boats, roasting corn and baking cakes, and tanning on the dock with a transistor radio growing out of her ear, listening to the peculiar music written for thirteen-year-old girls.

At the end of her thirteenth summer we did not return to Philadelphia. We went abroad instead because none of us spoke a foreign language and had never lived in Europe. We thought it high time that we did; that it would be good for us, good for the writing, and good for Victoria. I was sure that anyone could skip any grade in America without any loss at all if the year were to be filled with a compensatory value, and that for Victoria to live in a foreign country, attending the local school without knowing a word of its language, would be a considerable educational experience, if not an educational adventure. For that matter, we looked forward to adventure of our own: moving sight unseen to something we could not possibly anticipate, totally ignorant of Italy, its customs, and the names of its foods. Off we went with an English-Italian dictionary and phrase books that taught us to try to say, "Where are the javelins of my grandfather?"

When we returned to the river a year later the whole world had become a very different place for all of us and would never be the same again, for we now had different means of measurement. Fluent in Italian, fashionable in a miniskirt, and convinced of her womanhood by the attentions Italian males pay to every girl above age twelve, Victoria had undergone a sea change. And all of us, after having lived among evidence that life need not be a manic blur and that cities can be habitable, stared curiously at the highway billboards of our native land.

Yet the river seemed exactly the same, as if nothing had changed, as if time had not passed, as if we had never been away. Stretching to the horizons, it was wide and deep and as blue as the Italian sea we had lived beside. We returned on a warm bright day in June to the river serene and silent and to long, light days and languorous nights. As we neared our island a boat came out to intercept us, towing a raft. The Rahe boys were in the boat, and on the raft were poles holding up an old white bedspread with red letters painted on it. "Welcome Home Victoria," the letters said. That was something else that had not changed—or so it seemed.

12

Summer has a way of ending when you do not think it has, or should have ended, and you are always surprised to find it gone. Boats have the same stealthy way of leaving you, too, and one summer day we found the cypress outboard, which had been a sailboat before my wife was a child, which Will had modified, which Bob Bodine had loaned us when we bought the island, and which our children had painted scarlet and used as their school bus, was foundered to its gunwales in the boat slip. The white plywood outboard, purchased the year we bought the island, was beginning to leak around the transom and the bow.

There were fewer guests in summer now, and therefore we no longer had a constant need for three boats. We would need two, however, for as Will had said years ago, no one should live on an island with just one boat. What we needed was an inboard launch with a cabin on her for use in stormy weather. If we could replace the two outboards with a cabin launch, then, we told each other, we should. We looked around the river for such a launch and asked people in Rockport to help us find one. Ed Andress' workmen were repairing just the kind of boat we wanted.

"The fellow that bought her paid twelve hundred for her," one of the workmen said. "But, oh, there's a lot of work to do on her. There's a lot we done already you can't see; we had to put all new knees in her. And all along here we'll have to tear out and make over."

"She'll be a new boat when you're through," I said.

"Oh, yes, she will," he said. "And she'll cost something, too. Why, she's already got two hundred dollars' worth of new bronze screws in her, and we're not at the end of that yet."

That boat was not for sale. Her owner was having her restored for his own use; but the total cost to him was a nasty thought to bear in mind as we continued to look about. There were no new wooden launches for sale. To build a new one would be prohibitively expensive for us even though the Andress shop would be glad to do it at the fairest possible price; and if we could find an old launch within our means, the owner would doubtless have good reasons for agreeing to sell at the price we could pay.

We next thought of replacing the two outboards

with a new wooden one, but this would not give us the cabin we wanted. Even more to the point, there were no new wooden ones to buy. No one was making them any-more—not even out of plywood.

"What you need is one like this, JK," said Gerald Huck, who was in charge of sales at his father's marina.

Margaret and I stared numbly at the inboard-outboard that Gerry showed us. It was a big, beamy craft with a cabin on it, and new it cost more than a small house.

"That," I said, "is the last thing we need, Gerry."

"It isn't even a boat," Margaret said. "It's made of plastic."

Gerry smiled indulgently.

"We're talking about no upkeep," he reminded her. "We're talking about no caulking, no painting. We're talking about no dry rot."

"Let's talk about something we can buy," I suggested. "Margie thinks boats should be made of wood."

Gerry shrugged. "To be perfectly honest with you, JK," he said, "I don't think you're going to find what you want. If I knew where there was the boat you want, I'd tell you where it was."

We talked for a while about what we could not have, and then about what we needed in terms of use, and next about money.

Gerry understood everything we said. Like his fa-ther Ed Huck, he respected old craft too and sympa-thized with our distaste without wholly sharing it. He also knew from years past the modest size of our purse and he wanted to help us.

"Let me show you something," he said.

In the new sales showroom that was now a feature of the boatyard where Gerry's grandfather had designed and built by hand the gasoline engine that had powered old Mr. Weeks' launch, there was a fourteen-foot runabout with a windscreen and a buggy top and a 40-horsepower outboard engine astern. Once upon a time, an outboard was something you could put in the back trunk of a car. To lift one of the new ones you needed a chain falls, if not the use of the Brooklyn Navy Yard dock crane. I looked at it with disbelief. Margaret looked as dubiously at the bucket seats.

"You'll never have upkeep with this," Gerry said, returning to a favorite theme, "and you'll have plenty of power when you want it. If you want a covered boat, you just put up the buggy top and snap on the side curtains."

We said we would think it over.

"I tell you what, JK," he said. "I'll bring one out to the island tomorrow morning and you and Margie can try it out for yourselves."

The next morning was gray and calm and the plastic runabout hissed over the water at speed, its engine quiet enough for you to hear water bubbling under its planing hull. It started electrically. When you pushed forward on a throttle like an airplane's, the boat mounted onto its planing step and you flew over the river. I turned in a tight circle to cross the boat's slight wake, and the resulting jolt was felt from coccyx to skullcap. We talked about waves with Gerry, but he said we'd never get wet because the boat would go so fast we would leave the spray astern. I thought that this might be true enough, but instead of having a wet shirt you'd have a broken spine.

Margaret said it gave her a sinking feeling in the pit of her stomach even to think about buying that thing. Victoria, who was visiting with us, had another opinion.

"Buy it," she said. "Are you going to buy it, Dad?"

Although she would be on the island only for a weekend, Tory looked down a golden vista of endless summertime to see herself speeding around the river. She was a sunny, gregarious child who had none of her brother's solemnity and little of her sister's delicate precision. She flew into whatever she did. She liked to cook and did well at it, but by the time she was through in the kitchen there would be batter on the walls and flour in her ears from the way she beat a cake. She introduced the Rahe boys to jumping off the Yeo Island cliffs. While she was an emerging young woman with a flair for dress and a sensitivity to the moods of others, there was also much of the girl who had never worn shoes in any summer of her life and who was the happy child racing other children for the hundreds of gaily colored balloons that Rod Rahe had scattered on the river to make a water game for his son's birthday party. Victoria loved her name, and her approach to life indicated her complete agreement with the proposition that winning is a matter of getting there firstest with the mostest. In answer to her mother's question who would run that plastic kidney-breaker if we did buy it, Tory favored us with a charming smile.

My feeling was that we were back to Square One, if not behind it. My aversion to the runabout had to do with control. The whole point and charm of living on an island is that you are in control of all that goes on, and that whatever is done you do for yourself. If you want light, you set out the candles and fill the lamps with the oil. If you want something to eat, you can catch it out of the river and pick it from the fields. If you wish to be amused, you can amuse yourselves. An island is not so much an escape from an interdependent society as it is an experience of independence within manageable terms. On an island, you can do for yourself what you would have to allow others to do for you if you lived in a city. At the same time, you are free only to become your own slave, because everything you do takes time and effort. You therefore live slowly. This, I think, is what is meant by the phrase *the slower pace* of rural life. But in living more slowly, your time expands sufficiently for you to savor and enjoy what you are doing and to take deep pleasure in what you have done. The only events and forces beyond your control are natural ones—as lawyers say, acts of God. You then do what you can with your intelligence and skill to cope with winds and water, and there is more fierce joy to be found in this than there is in telephoning for a taxi when it rains.

It is just here that the plastic boats represented something beyond my control. They had been created by people who wanted to make money in a mass market. Their success demonstrates Gresham's law: The shoddy will always drive the good out of such a market. The appearance of plastic had pushed wood into the tiny and special market reserved for the rich. Money-making had invaded my river, narrowed my choices, diminished my pleasure, and had taken something away from my summer—wholly apart from the much more serious damage it had done to an ancient craft and worthwhile skills and the still more serious damage it was doing to human lives.

The boats were dangerous, because a boat like Gerry's lacked forward visibility till you brought it up on its planing step—to do so at night meant that you would have to drive much faster than was safe, and if you struck a log you could very well go through the glass windscreen. Moreover, the sternlight reflected into the windscreen, totally robbing you of visibility forward. For this reason, many people who drove such boats would switch off their running lights at night and thus convert their craft into unseen projectiles dangerous to others.

Doubtless this lack of visibility, the sternlight glaring into the windscreen, put an end to summer for six young people whose boat exploded onto a small, low island not much larger than a shoal. Impaled on the steering column, the driver died. A young woman was hurled at perhaps forty miles an hour onto the island, breaking her pelvis. Only one man got out with nothing broken. It may of course be argued that the people, not the boat, were responsible for this disaster, but the boat had a great deal to do with it. The boat was shaped by money, not by a boatwright, and what happened that night was a sacrifice to Mammon, and we were among its victims.

We were left with two alternatives: We could either buy one of Gerry's new runabouts, accepting its discomfort and its potential dangerousness, or we could extensively rebuild our two wooden outboard motorboats. In neither case would we have the cabin launch we wanted and needed. We meanwhile needed a seaworthy second boat, and we needed one then and there, not some months later when the outboards would be replanked, caulked, painted, and taken up. I am ashamed to say that we bought that overpowered runabout, to Victoria's incredulous joy.

Child of a new age, she mastered the pushbutton controls with the speed of light. In the days before she returned to the city, she was scarcely ashore for a longer time than it took to fill the gasoline tanks. She shot around the river with a singular *éclat*, and when she came screaming toward the boathouse she would chop the throttle at just the microsecond that would mush the boat down into the water to bring it gliding gently into the narrow boat slip without touching on either side. The boat seemed to suit her abilities so exactly that we named it the *Tory* and told her it was hers. She left for the city saying she could hardly wait to come back to the river when her typing courses were over.

We, however, felt a certain sense of loss. Not only was the plastic boat something extra-insular, forced upon us, an intruder over whom we had no control, but it represented the end of a valuable tradition having to do with wood, wind, and water. No doubt sailormen resented the dawn of the age of steam for exactly this reason. In fact, I have met some who still do, although they have no personal knowledge of full-rigged ships. I know how they feel. They feel that some part of man's summer has needlessly slipped away.

There were, however, other opinions.

"Why didn't you get us a boat like that when we were kids?" our son wanted to know when he appeared for a weekend visit.

His sister Margaret was equally enchanted to discover the *Tory* when she arrived.

"I thought you two would never buy a plastic boat," she said. Although she did not particularly care to drive it, any more than she cared for driving anything else, she did love to ride in the *Tory,* enjoying its bouncing speed.

Our older children, like Victoria, immediately recognized something that belonged to their age, not to ours. They understood the boat's disadvantages and accepted them. If you wanted to see at night, all you had to do was kneel on the driver's seat cushion with your head above the windscreen. To see in a rain, the driver would have to get wet, his head poking through a turned-back corner of the buggytop. To handle the boat, you had to remember she was too light and to make allowance for this fact in a wind. Like Victoria, the older children needed only the fraction of an instant to understand everything about the operation of the *Tory.* They viewed our complaints tolerantly enough. We were after all members of a former generation. In our family, the generations were not at war, perhaps because the island had made us allies in years past, but we were different. Our children were pleasantly surprised to find that we had finally shown a little good sense when it came to buying a new boat.

13

"When do you think she'll be ready?" I asked Ed Andress.

"Oh, she'll be ready in August," the old man said. "So she's getting married, eh?"

He paused to think about this, leaning on his elbows on the counter of his Rockport post office. The little room was hot with the coal stove going; there was steam on the windows.

"I can remember when she wasn't high enough to see over the counter," he said, peering over it to see a child. "Seems it wasn't any time ago. And now she's getting married. Well, there'll be a lot of good times and sad stories.

"Oh, we'll have her in, all right," he said, straightening up. "You want to see her? She's up the hill in the shed."

He pulled a Mackinaw over his bib overalls, and we went up the hill to look at her. Ed leaned into the hill; all the Andress family did that, leaning at an angle parallel with the steep slope that rose behind the post office and charging up it, and Old Eddie, as many of the people called him, could climb his hill as briskly as any of them for all his more than eighty years.

"You're building her upside down?" I wondered, looking at the vast hull in the cold and empty shed.

"Why, yes," he said. "We'll build her decks when we get her in the water."

He explained that when the hull was built, they would slide her down the hill on rollers, with tractors astern to act as brakes, and they'd put her in upside down and turn her over in the river. It would be better to turn her in the water, Ed thought, than to turn her over on land, because when you had her weight on one gunwale, the land wouldn't give but the water would.

"Then we'll pump her out and build her decks," he said.

"And she'll be ready by August?" Margaret wanted to know.

"Oh yes, I guess she will, if I can find the men," Ed promised.

There was no one working on her now, in the very early spring, and the hull of the tour boat was far from finished. There would be engines and shafts to install, two decks to be built, seats to be put in place; the ship had to be fitted out, the sea trials held, and the license granted. I thought that it would be a close-run thing, and it would be very awkward to try to make last-minute arrangements in the very crescendo of the tourist season if that boat was not ready. When we asked the Rockport Boat Line if we could charter a boat for the wedding party, this was the one they said we could have. She was being built to a new design, and apart from being proud of that, they wanted us to have their newest boat because, they said, it would be the first time there had ever been a wedding party on a tour boat.

We left Ed Andress with a hope for the best of luck, and thus began The Summer of the Weddings. It was the shortest summer of our lives, because it was the fullest of them all—a time of goings and comings that began with three graduations in three different places. Our daughter Margaret was graduated from the University of Pennsylvania; Christopher and his fiancée Wendy from Harvard; our daughter Victoria from high school. I finished one book and started another, and next there was Christopher's and Wendy's wedding in June.

We drove down to Long Island for that and discovered a pretty church set among great trees and flowers, cool in the warm sunlight, and a lawn full of handsome young people and the happiness of everyone on a marriage day. More than a banquet, the wedding luncheon was a feast. When at last the rice was thrown and Chris and Wendy set off in a car whose hubcaps their friends had filled with noisy pebbles, we made our way back to the river to prepare for our daughter Margaret's nuptials two months hence and to watch, anxiously, the slow construction of what we were calling the wedding barge.

We were glad that Margaret wanted to be married on the river rather than in Philadelphia, for it was a way of telling us that she, too, regarded the river as her home. The people of Rockport and our island friends assured us that it was. The Rockport parish gave us permission to use their Anglican church, and our friend, Halsey Cook, an Anglican priest from Baltimore, whose summer island is near our own, volunteered to perform the ceremony and obtained the necessary ecclesiastical permission to officiate in another priest's parish. Gordon Davidson, who was a Canadian lawyer, cut twenty miles of red tape in order that two American citizens could marry in Canada. The Rahes volunteered to give breakfast to the bridegroom, Kirk Jenne, and to his brother Frank, who would be best man. The Rahe boys promised to serve as a water taxi. Boys from Rockport, who had helped us with carpentry in summers past, wanted to direct traffic when the wedding guests arrived. Kate and Bob Bodine invited everyone to a lawn party the evening before the wedding. Margaret's cousins, Susannah and Cornelia, promised to play the organ and the oboe and suggested that nothing could be more appropriate for a river wedding than Handel's *Wasser-Musik*. Our contribution, apart from listening to this orchestra of voluntary activity rather than having to direct it, was to polish the brass Crucifix and candlesticks, help to arrange the flowers in the church, and hope that we would not find a battery dead when it came time to cross the river. We were given the parish register to keep overnight. This horrified Gordon. A vestryman in his church in Montreal and a lawyer besides, he protested that a parish register was a legal document that must at all times be in the custody of the parish. We were very pleased. To be trusted was to be made welcome at home.

The day was bright and fair, a perfect river day. Two hours before the ceremony, the bride and her sister were barefoot girls with newly washed, stringy hair, dressed in sweatshirts and shorts made of old blue jeans, interestedly watching the huge black bass cruising slowly in the clear water past the stavings of our dock. In this costume they and their mother walked up Rockport's street to the motel next to the church, where Mrs. Allen, who ran the motel, asked, unbelievingly, "This is the bride?"

There ensued a period of female hysteria about which I later learned. Two towers of strength combined to save the situation. One was Wendy, calm and serene, who ironed the attendants' dresses when Victoria seemed too nervous to do it. The other was Peter Davidson, that practical Down Easter who was prepared for any emergency. From her handbag she produced a scissors to trim the stems of the flowers which would otherwise be taller than the Crucifix. When at the eleventh hour it was discovered that my wife had forgotten her brooch, Peter dived into her handbag to produce a stunningly appropriate one. Also from her commodious and completely equipped purse she extracted a small bottle of whisky to steady the nerves of the mother of the bride.

"I thought you might need it," she said, pouring a thimbleful for herself as well. The bride, lost in a trance of her own, was oblivious to all this.

When Handel filled the church and the summer air, I lent my daughter an arm.

"I'm going to be married! I'm going to be married!" she said as we climbed the three steps into the little brown wooden country chapel.

She seemed to want to gallop to the altar, and I sought to restrain the pace at least to a sedate canter.

The altar brass gleamed in the light falling through the tinted windows; the flowers glowed against the dark, pine-paneled walls. Halsey was a commanding presence; the bridegroom had that air of earnest seriousness that bridegrooms have. Down the aisle past Jim and Hazel Wallace and Agnes Khant and the Creightons and Will's son Edson and his wife Mildred; past the Bodines and friends from Philadelphia and Rockport and the children's friends from college, although I suppose you could not call any of them children now; past Rockport people and city people and summer people, all of whom had had a part in shaping into a woman the maiden who now wore her mother's bridal gown. And the sound of water music for a river-daughter.

The receiving line was arranged along the Rockport Boat Line's dock, and the wedding guests, walking down the little hill from the church, passed along the line and aboard the wedding barge—newly through its sea trials, bright in its new paint, and ready as Ed Andress had guessed she might be, just in time. She was flying flags the Davidsons had provided: the Union Jack for the

Commonwealth; the Canadian maple leaf; the American flag for us; and the Red Lion of Scotland in honor of the bridegroom and his clan.

The way upriver led past memories of all the summers; the remembered fishing grounds of dawns and evenings; familiar trees and points of land; past the Indian falling from the cliff; into the swift whirlpools beneath the bridge; through the Lost Channel into the island maze; and so to Glen House, a lodge at river's edge, on whose broad porch a champagne luncheon awaited us. When it came time for the bridal pair to leave us, they ran down the lawn through the rice to the river, where there was a boat to take them on their separate journey. The rest of us returned to Rockport on the wedding barge in the long low light of a late-August afternoon on the last day of summer.

It was the last day of summer because the next day was cold, with the first steel clouds of fall and the river gray and empty in the wind. It was also the last day of the summer of our lives on the river, and we were glad to have it so and glad that it had been a day of greens and blues and gold, with songs and wine and flags flying in celebration of an end and a beginning on a river that moves, and changes, and remains the same without beginning or end.

PART FOUR

Fall

14

When the world begins to follow its winter path around the sun, winds and weathers spill through the Thousand Islands, bringing us a dank time that smells of damp wood, sodden wool, forest mold, rain, and wood-smoke. Midday may be too dark to read and write, and your mood may fall as low as the barometer. There is not much fun in fishing and boating. In this rain, the last tourists look entirely miserable, swimming is out of the question, the river is falling, the summer people disappear, and the swallows wisely leave our boathouse to prolong their summer elsewhere.

We are always of two minds about the swallows. They make a mess of the boathouse and its boats, but we love their skidding, veering flight, and vastly enjoy watching the nestlings grow and learn to fly. When the weather turns sour and the swallows leave, we are doubly conscious of a sense of loss: the loss of our birds and the loss of summer. We also have mixed feelings about this season that is not a season but a gray sogginess of empty time the natives call Squaw Winter. It is an unattractive, dispiriting nuisance, but if we did not have it, and have it early, we would not have the full glory of fall. In those years when the rains do not come and when summer holds on and on through September, and one golden clear hot day succeeds another, there will be no color. The leaves will simply turn dull, brown, and dry and fall as they do in Europe. For color a fortnight of soaking rain is needed at summer's end, while it is still warm and the leaves still green. Then a sudden frost. After this, the weather can turn as clear and fine as you please, but the leaves will be brilliant and stay on the trees throughout October.

The sumacs are the first to become red flame in fall. Next, the birches are hung with little golden hearts. After them, first one and next several branches of a maple take fire until all the maples are wholly orange and scarlet. I have seen Vermont in fall and it is remarkable, but the river in fall, and the back country to the north beyond, are magical. On a still, clear October day you look from our island across a luminous deep-blue river to see on farther islands the silver and gold of the birches and the reds, yellows, and oranges of the hardwoods, against the dark green of the conifers, and farther yet the glowing horizon of Canadian mainland lying beneath the washed blue in the west and north. There is a perfect silence in the early morning now that the tourists and the campers have gone and the cottages of the summer people are empty. A faint wind on a still fall morning may carry distant sounds into your silence: the chunking of an unseen ore ship's propellor in the Seaway; the far whistle of a train somewhere crossing the Canadian mainland; the dull double thuds of a duck hunter's gun in the marsh at the foot of Grenadier Island. Otherwise, you are alone in a silent world painted in still fires; alone with your wife, with the muskrat that leaves a quiet wake as it swims with its weeds and twigs to its house beneath your dock, and with the Great Blue Heron standing still on a stone at water's edge. You have the long golden sunlight, the colors, the silences, and the river to yourselves. Rockport becomes a village again, with only the workboats of the rivermen moored at its docks.

"This here is our summer," a Rockport man told me. "With all those people out of here, we can have some time to ourselves."

He said this at a time when there were still summer people's cottages to be shuttered for winter and their boats to be taken out of the water, but neither he nor anyone else in Rockport was scurrying about these labors. It was a time for sitting on the store steps, or tilting a chair against a boathouse wall in a sunny lee; a time for apples, cider, pumpkins, duck hunting, visiting, and sleeping well through frosty nights. It was also a time for fishing, for the fish are firm and heavy in fall, feeding hungrily against the chill that has come to the steadily lowering river. The summer water weeds die and disappear, and it is possible to troll again in the old, favorite places. If after the rains and an early frost there is a splendor among the trees, there is also likely to be a time of perfect weather that sometimes extends into December. During the shortening days the sunlight is bright, though gradually cooling, and sometimes there are light falls of snow.

October is usually the best of the fall months. In a lee, the sun still has much of summer's weight in it, and you can sunbathe in eighty degrees of warmth reflected by the white walls of your boathouse, or work in the mornings in the cottage at the head of the island while wearing only a shirt. Although there is almost never a wind after dark, still it is cold, and on full-moon October nights, dressed against the chill, Margaret and I drift slowly in the current among the islands, to see in flooding moonlight the colors of the island forests both above the island rocks and below, perfectly mirrored in the quiet water. Twisting veils or wisps of vapor pour off the red and green running lights, the varnished decks sop with dew, and often enough shafts and curtains of light pulsate and ripple in the north. Waiting for us at the island is the warmth of rock maple burning slowly on the hearth, and later the comfort of that deep swallow's nest of blankets and tufted quilt.

October is pre-eminently the month of Indian summer. The original connotations of this term were fearsome and grisly, for it was in this time of perfect weather that the aboriginal warriors of the region went raiding south into the settlements of the Mohawk Valley. Now that the savages have been vanquished and therefore ennobled, the term has taken on a tone of poignant romance that our pioneer ancestors would not have understood, but whether it is called Indian summer by whatever meaning of the term, or their summer, as the Rockport people call it, October is no kind of summer at all. It is fall.

In the years since our older children married and Victoria left high school to continue her education in Rome, Margaret and I have been alone on our island in the long glory of fall. For the first time in our lives we have been free to arrive on the river as early as we wished and able to stay as late as we pleased.

"You mean you stay here all fall?" a woman asked. "I know it must be pretty then, because fall is pretty, don't you think? But it is lonely, isn't it? I mean, with everybody gone and nobody to talk to."

Since she wanted me to agree with her, I was tempted to say "Yes." But since the truth of the matter was "No," I hunted around for a way of saying so, in terms she could understand. If I said it was impossible for me to feel lonely anywhere I had my wife and my work, that would be only part of the truth and a rather sententious bit of it at that. To explain the rest of it would take too long for the purposes of our cocktail-party conversation, held on a friend's dock one afternoon at summer's end.

"Let me get you another of those delicious sandwiches," I said.

By the time I returned she was talking with someone else, which is the one great advantage of a cocktail party, and I joined in what they were saying.

The complete explanation would have included a distinction between being alone and being lonely and the notion that the loneliness of the river in fall is indeed among its charms. It is a time of year when the river resumes those features that attracted us to the region twenty years ago. Of course the river has changed in certain ways since then. The water is not so clean as it was. There are more cottages in the area, more tourists in summer, and there are now street lights in the village of Rockport. In recent summers the local canvas has become somewhat overcharged. What was once a rural landscape by Pieter Breughel now rather resembles the Fourth of July at a New Jersey lake as painted by Hieronymus Bosch. But Squaw Winter comes to blow the tourists and the plastic yachtsmen off the river, and we are again given the peace and simplicity we first found here. We are alone but not, as the woman at the cocktail party presumed, lonely.

When she supposed there would be no one to talk to, she of course meant there would be no one like herself with whom we could discuss the affairs of the civilized world. She knew we belonged to that world and thought we would be lonely for it. The complete answer, which I could not possibly have explained at that time, is no, but she was right to think that our position in Rockport's scheme of things was somewhat anomalous. Like our island itself, which rises out of Canadian water only a hundred yards or so within the Canadian side of the International Line, we are barely within the gates—not as strangers but surely as guests.

Margaret and I will never reach the center of village

life. You would have to be born and raised and to live all your life in Rockport to do that. But after twenty years of living on our island at least part if not most of each year, we do have a place of sorts in the community. When news spread that thieves had clubbed Mrs. Heffernan unconscious, one of the Rockport women told Margaret, "None of the local people would have done that. It must have been some of the summer people." The point was put again when we were entrusted with a secret. "Now I can tell you folks," we were told, "but I can't say anything about it to the people around here." Evidently we were not regarded as either locals or as summer people. We are, however, often regarded as translators.

"You know the Jepsons, don't you?" a man in a marina asked me.

"Yes, I've met them," I said.

"Well, Jepson, he says he wants this and he wants that, and he comes tearing in here this morning like he had a bee up his pants, and I told him, 'Mr. Jepson, we've ordered your new timer from Kingston but it hasn't got here yet.' So he leans back all high and mighty and says, 'Well, why don't you go to Kingston and get it? It's only thirty miles away.'

"Now how the hell can we do that when we've got only one mechanic and neither of us can get away? We've got all we can do, and Jepson, he doesn't have a goddam thing to do except come up here and fish."

"Why don't you tell him to go to Kingston and fetch it himself?"

"Well, if I told you that, that's what you'd do, JK, because you know how it is here. But him . . ."

"You want me to suggest it to Jepson?"

"By gee, it would be fine if you would, JK. You'd know how to talk to him, but when he comes tearing in here we just squeak on each other."

Living in the region late in the fall, we and Rockport friends gossip and fish and share meals and mutually discover the patterns of our lives to be remarkably similar. Still, there are differences that will always prevent a complete sharing, and these are the same kinds of differences that separate families, neighborhoods, states, nations, races, and city people from country people.

"I don't read books," one woman said. "My mother never would let me read books when I was a girl. She said if you read a book all morning, you don't have anything to show for the time you spent, but if you bake a pie or work on a quilt, why, then you do."

She said this neither sadly nor proudly, but simply stating a divisive fact. She spoke out of one background to people of another. Another divisive fact is nationality. It would be difficult to find two people more alike than the English Canadians and the English Americans. We were in fact once the same people, for British Ontario, as the Canadians sometimes call it, was largely settled by fugitives from the terror of the American Revolution— by those who remained loyal to the Crown. Their descendants call themselves United Empire Loyalists with the same pride that the descendants of the terrorists call themselves the Sons and Daughters of the American Revolution. Two hundred years later, a division exists, because we are no longer the same people for all the talk of our common heritage and undefended mutual frontier. You can have a Canadian friend, and he can see in you an American friend, but history will have placed a national qualification on your friendship. Religion, too, can be a bar to sharing. Effie Slate refused to attend a wedding in her family because the girl was "marrying a Frenchman." For her, the Battle of the Boyne was just as compelling as it is in Ireland today; in addition to her Scots-Irish descent, Effie also carried a racial memory of the French and Indian Wars. If we had ever spoken of religion with Will and Effie, our relationship would have been very different.

We share with Rockport people all the many things that can be shared, and so far as human companionship is concerned, we are certainly not lonely. But we are nevertheless aware of a separating difference, and we become particularly aware of it in the fall—not only because fall is a time for gathering-in and storing-up and taking stock, and because we know we have entered the fall of our lives, but also because we must begin to think in fall of where we might spend the winter. We do not have an ice boat, and when ice comes to the river you cannot live on an island without one. More to the point, when winter comes, we are as ready as the swallows for a change of scene, glad to leave the country for the city.

If our position in Rockport is somewhat anomalous, however, so is our position anywhere else. I am sure the island made it so. For the past twenty years the island, immobile and timeless, has been the one constant, fixed point of reference in our lives. Over the years the island became our native land, and our family became our nation. This made the outside world larger and more various, while at the same time it allowed us to view all other nations impartially. We now say "the Americans" exactly as we would say "the Malays" or "the French," and view the activities and customs of our erstwhile countrymen with the same lively interest we take in the Italians when we are in their country, or in the Igorots when we are in theirs. During those twenty years when we were establishing a fixed base in our lives, the island was preparing us to be free to enter the world.

Now we live in Europe in winter. We are not at home abroad in the sense that we are not Europeans and never will be. But we are not precisely tourists. Europe is not a place we visit but our winter habitat, and for all that language, customs and beliefs remain a barrier to communication and that our residence abroad is brief and superficial, we feel more at home there than we do in the United States.

We are as much alone in Europe in winter as we are upon our island in fall, and there are fewer people with whom we can talk and share good times than there are in Rockport, because we arrive as strangers and leave before acquaintance can be much improved. We have, however, a considerable practice in self-sufficiency behind us, so although we are alone, we are not lonely. More important, we feel at the very heart of civilization, which is something we cannot feel in the United States. When I walk along the Arno and see the graceful lines of the palaces along the river and Giotto's tower and the tower of the Palazzo Vecchio rising behind them, and when I then turn to walk through narrow medieval streets, the effect is somewhat different from that of walking in any American city you might want to mention. And what is true of Florence is largely true of many cities in Europe: Someone has cared. Beauty and tradition are honored and preserved. No one has torn down the Pantheon to raise a parking garage on the site. There is a concern for affairs of the mind and for works of art, for manners, dress, deportment, and civility. There seems to me to be a greater tolerance of human frailty as well, although understanding might be the better word for it. There is, in sum, a quality of humanism in Europe that I, for one, find missing in the United States. A friend explained it thus: In France, the man is free, but the citizen is not; in the United States, the citizen is free, but the man is not. Perhaps so. My view may be sentimental because it is superficial, but I think a sense of history lies at the core of European experience which helps the populace to discriminate between the valuable and the shoddy and helps, too, to provide an emotional stability that seems to me to be missing in America. The political gyrations of the Europeans are as unimportant as our own; what is important is the quality of life.

These thoughts may be the cackling of an aging grandfather, rocking on the porch of his island home, complaining that they don't make things these days like they used to, and the country's going to hell what with the way people are behaving and that gang they have in the White House. However this may be, I am trying to answer the question the woman raised at the cocktail party.

Yes, we need the city in our lives.

But the city to us is not a particular one. It is rather

the city of man, where the arts of civilization are prac-
ticed. We have found this city not only in Florence and
Rome but in London and in the ancient town of Sandwich and in the fishing village of Porto Santo Stefano,
where much of this book was written.

We are alone both on the island and in Europe and
are now apparently separated if not divorced from our
native land. We are as apparently migratory as the swallows in our boathouse. I cannot say that our lives would
not have taken the shape they did if we had not bought
the island twenty years ago. Yet, an island is a curious
thing with mysterious powers. It can, it seems, isolate
you, then turn you into a bird.

15

Canada sent us a greeting one fall morning, just after dawn, in the form of Morris Huck, bearded like Captain Ahab, who came to our dock in an olive-drab outboard.

"Hey, JK," he said, "what are you doing up so early?"

It was a teasing that implied my countrymen did nothing and slept late.

"I wondered who was doing that shooting," I said. "Was that you?"

"Well, I guess it was," Morris said. "I got something for you."

He reached down and held up two mallard hens. They were beautiful birds, nearly as large as chickens.

He steered into the boat slip, and I could see other ducks on the floorboards of his outboard. He had shot them from a blind on an island quite near ours, and we talked about the weather and the birds and going out together to shoot one morning. Morris was one of Ed Huck's sons. The Hucks were a large family who could have eaten all the ducks in the boat, but Morris wanted us to have two of them. I thanked him very much.

"Oh, that's O.K.," Morris said. "Margaret will have a feather picking, and you'll have a duck dinner."

We laughed and waved goodbye as Morris set off for his home on the mainland.

Although he did not know it, Morris had given us more than a pair of ducks. He had given us an unexpected holiday on a day in fall—another part of the complicated reason why we prefer to live on our island at this time of year.

We spent the morning on the dock, plucking the birds and cleaning them for roasting, carefully working out the pinfeathers. We could coat the birds with paraffin, and, when it has cooled, strip off the wax and the pinfeathers would come with it, but I have always felt this tends to make a duck taste like candle ends and that it is better to spend an hour and more plucking by hand. We saved the feathers and down for pillows and the iridescent pinions for decoration.

The Canadians like to cut ducks like frying chickens and sauté them in a pan. Our preference is to stuff them with a mixture of yams and apples, roast them, and dress them with sliced oranges. Wild ducks mean a feast, not a supper. Morris' mallard hens were young and firm-fleshed, without a trace of fat. They would taste no more like those greasy commercial blobs known as Long Island ducklings than a chop cut from a wild Tuscan boar would taste like one from a placid, overfed Iowa hog. They would be a feast, but feasts, like ducks, require a bit of preparation, involving friends and wine.

Having no telephone, we could not call the Creightons to see if they would be free that evening, but they were islanders who lived as we did—in a way that permitted us all to drop whatever we were doing to enjoy an unexpected occasion. They, too, kept time by the season rather than by the minute. While I worried with the last of the pinfeathers, Margaret went downriver to ask Bill and Marty to dinner.

It was nearly noon when she returned. There had been the miles down to the Creightons' island and a chat there, and on the way back Margaret stopped at Rockport for apples and yams. There she had met Morris Huck's mother, Cassie, who said there was no reason to buy apples when there were more McIntoshes on the ground under her tree than she had time to make into applesauce for herself, but mind the yellowjackets when you go to gather them; there were two nests right by the tree and bees all over the apples. The ladies visited while they gathered apples and put them in a carton and debated the various ways of preparing ducks until it was time to talk about buying yams and wonder who might have some. Margaret returned from her morning on the river with ten gallons of gasoline, a box of apples, a can of yams, and the Creightons' acceptance. Lunch was a hurried affair, for time was moving through our timeless day. While Margaret cooked her yams and apples, I crossed the river and drove through the brilliance of the back-country foliage to the village of Lansdowne to buy wine at the liquor store. The trip was as hurried as lunch, because the days are short in fall, and since we did not have electricity or lamps for the kitchen, we would have an early dinner at sunset. It would be too cold to eat on the dining porch, and so there would be the living room to rearrange as a dining room, a coal fire to start in the Quebec heater, and a fire to build on the hearth. There was the dining table to set, hors d'oeuvres to prepare, the living-room oil lamps to trim and fill—and then a bath (which meant running the pump) and a change into cleaner, if no more formal, clothes.

Morris' gift of ducks at dawn had pushed work aside and filled a day with pleasant busyness that came gliding smoothly to a stop in the last long golden light of late afternoon. A black shape appeared on the burnished water, coming toward us off the head of Yeo Island. We recognized the Creightons' boat by its outline. By the time we were on the dock we could see its color, Bill at the wheel forward, and Marty in the stern sheets ready to throw us a line.

There followed a familiar, comfortable ritual born years ago out of the difficulty of landing a boat in the current and wind that comes along our dock. Glad as we were to see our guests, their boat's need came first. We took their lines and cleated them. Bill handed up the flashlights they would later need and the extra boat coats. Marty put a carton on the dock containing fresh flowers and tomatoes from her garden and an apple strudel she had baked for our dessert. They arranged the tarpaulin over the boat cushions against the dew that would come with the dark and accepted a hand up out of the boat that lay low against the stavings at this time of low water. All this having been done in an efficient silence, we then said hello.

It had been cold on the water, but the living room was pleasant with two fires and with the waning sun warming the western wall and spilling through the windows and the scent of the hearth fire and the aroma from the kitchen. The ducks were as fine as they should have been, a kind of miniature harvest of the efforts of the day on a day in fall, and we lingered over the coffee in a room now lighted by the hearth, Aladdin lamps, the red glow of the Quebec heater, and candles on the supper table.

I am sure that we and the Creightons enjoyed spur-of-the-moment occasions, and one another's company, to a greater extent in the fall than we did when we dined together at one another's islands in summer. In the summer everything seems perhaps too easy; perhaps too much is taken for granted. But in the fall there is always a strange quality of excitement that gives the color of adventure to such a simple thing as sharing a brace of duck with friends. Like us, the Creightons are American guests of Canada who come early to their island in spring and leave late in fall, and when we visit one another so late in the year it is more like taking a voyage than a boat ride. The river, so full of boat lights and cottage lights on summer nights, is dark, cold, and still in fall. Once you leave the pale loom of our boathouse to steer toward passages among the black bulk of island masses, the only wink of light and warmth after long river miles is the Creightons' cottage at the foot of Tar Island. It seems more welcome then, and they more glad to see friends appear out of the surrounding night. Of course we have good times in summer, but in fall there is an additional mood—as of friends meeting quite by happy chance.

I think the quality of excitement in fall derives from an underlying feeling that whatever is done has a more direct relation to the future than whatever is done at any other season. Once we enjoyed almost too much excitement in simply loading two cords of oak into the *Margaret,* for the weight of it drew her down to her gunwales. Instead of prudently making two trips, we risked doing it in one, and all the way across the river from the mainland we crept dead slow, wondering at our foolishness and hoping no wind came up, thinking about those oak baulks sunk off Rockport in the nineteenth century. But that was the superficial excitement. The underlying one, the truly exciting one, was not this witlessly perilous crossing so much as it was storing the wood away in contemplation of the comfort we would know on cold nights and gale-ridden days.

During the first fall that Margaret and I were alone on the island, we puttered happily about the river in a new acquisition. The white plywood outboard hull had lasted a year or so longer than Will had predicted, but now it had to be replaced. For complex reasons associated with competitive economics, a loss of innocence resulting from the purchase of the plastic runabout, and the now tiresome task of patching and caulking and of trying to find paint that would hold wet boards together, we surrendered to progress and bought an unsinkable aluminum outboard hull painted a dull green. On this we hung the old five-horsepower outboard engine from the plywood hull and immediately rediscovered the great pleasure of moving slowly, down among the waves. The river, made larger in fall by the absence of other boats, became larger still now that we crept around it once again. Islands took a great long time to pass, and we saw much more of them as they went by; we saw the ripples lapping under stone ledges and heard the glunk of it, the sound that Margaret learned as a child. It meant that a hobgoblin lived there, she was told. Going among the waves in the aluminum boat was to return to a time when we were newly married. There had been two of us then with all of time before us (provided I survived the war), and now there were two of us again with all our time to fill as we pleased.

We moved slowly in a small boat upon a great river, trolling in the evening after work and rather hoping not to catch a fish too soon. Preparing to go fishing can be like preparing to go camping, in that much of the pleasure lies in making the preparations. You look at the sky for weather signs, decide where to fish by the direction of the wind, gather the clothes you will need, remember to take a flashlight, check the rods, lines, and baitboxes, make sure you have boat cushions, oars, and gasoline— and then at the last minute you remember the gill chain. In all this time you pleasantly anticipate the head-shaking tugging of something large and mysterious deep in the secret water and the first view of what has suddenly struck your bait and may now be seen deeply swimming toward the boat before it leaps or runs. Even if you catch no fish, you will have the pleasure of the boat ride.

But you are sometimes disappointed, as when after making your preparations the wind suddenly backs into the north and threatens to become a gale. And once, just as Margaret had begun to pay out line, a heavy pike took her bait not ten yards from the boathouse. The spoon was so far down its gullet that to extract the lure would kill the fish. We therefore had to keep the pike, and because the fish would be more than enough dinner for the two of us, we had to stop fishing before we had fairly started. We were delighted with our catch, but we had looked forward to an evening on the sunset water.

One bright October day we moved slowly downriver close along the outside flank of Grenadier Island. We followed the course toward Heffernan's till we saw the patch of green lawn beneath trees at the edge of the old Buell farm. That was an island cemetery, and we had long intended to visit it because, to us, country churchyards and country cemeteries have stories to tell. We ran ashore, beached the boat, made our way through brush and wild grapevines and emerged on the lawn beneath the trees.

It is a simple country graveyard lying by itself in an island forest with no house near. Several generations of five families are buried here. Effie Slate's family is one. Between the lines of names and dates graven on these old, flat stones you can read stories of long toils to create homes and livelihoods in the island forests of a cold northern land. There are tales of death at birth, of children lost, and of long lives of pioneers who survived their perilous infancies. You can also, on such a sun-filled October day as that of our visit, imagine the stories of simple joys, for these people, too, had known the deep clear water, the changing light of sun and clouds moving over islands, the sight of deer in fall at the edge of the farm, the flight of birds. No doubt such joys moved them to live here, of all places on earth, and abide its long winters of ice and storms. Now they are dead in the sunlight. Others care for the lawn, the stones and the trees, and preserve a clear view of the blue river, the low-lying islands offshore and the channel beyond. It is a good place to be dead if you lived on the river, and here we found Chuck Handley's grave.

We thought of Chuck's finding us the *Margaret* years ago and saw him laughing as he told us he had the same view the millionaires had. "Here we are," he said as we and our children ate with him and his family on the porch of his island house, "eating chicken and looking at the sunset, and if you had a million dollars it wouldn't make the chicken or the sunset any better, would it?" Chuck did not have a million dollars. He had a truck, and he would drive a load of goods from one city to another and bring a load back again and return to live on his island till the money ran out and he would have to climb back into the cab of his truck to earn another haulage fee. For a few days on the road he would earn weeks on the river, and the river was where he lived. A skilled mechanic,

Chuck could have worked every day of his life in a city garage and made a great deal more money, but then he would not have had the river and the view of the sunset from his island. Standing beside his grave, we quite agreed with his choice.

After all, there seems to be no objective meaning in human existence; life has only whatever meaning you choose to give it. But insofar as we may say that human life will persist, then we may say that so long as it does, some aspects of it are immortal. These will be whatever has moved men to love, grief, or joy in all man's time on earth. I do not know why so many people, particularly the Americans, have such a dread of death that they want to hear nothing about it and why, if they think of the dead at all, they must imagine them resting or sleeping or alive in some other world. Better to regard death as one of the facts of life, equally as important and as necessary as birth, and to regard the death of the individual as evidence of an ongoing process, timeless and immemorial. One of the ways of paying respect to life is burying the dead. People lived here, the graveyard said to me. It was wrong, I thought, to look down one's nose and write English poetry about the short and simple annals of the poor. Chuck had never been poor, and he certainly was not simple, and I dare say none of the others in that country graveyard were either. Evidently, what was important to them was the river, the islands, stones and trees: some leagues of peace, silence, solitude, and the sound of hobgoblins.

What remains to be seen is whether the living will be able to preserve those aspects of the region which led the Indians to call it the Garden Place of the Great Spirit. I am sure they would want the Garden available to their children till the end of time. But adaptable and self-reliant as the river people are, and attractive as a timeless rural and aquatic life may be, the river population is small and, politically speaking, relatively unsophisticated as well. There are, moreover, other attractions and, more important, other people. The region is not at some far end of the earth; it is within a day's drive of Montreal, Toronto, Philadelphia, New York, Boston, Detroit, Cleveland, Pittsburgh and all the smaller cities between. The Seaway passes through it now, and it is the nature of sea captains to clean their ships by throwing their filth over the side and, despite regulations and the possibility of being caught and fined, to blow out their oily bilges into water that people drink, killing fish and ducks as well. There is little the people of Rockport can do to compel the larger towns on the riverbanks and the cities on the Great Lakes to stop pouring their untreated sewage into the common water. If the Garden is to be preserved, the local population will need help. Much is forthcoming; more has been promised; the river when compared to others is only barely tainted and may soon return to its original air-clear quality if all the promised help arrives and all goes well. Recently enacted Canadian regulations are evidently having their effect, because the Canadian channel is clearing now. The most recent test showed the count of bioforms per milliliter to be zero in the water around our island, and, for the first time in the last five years, the government report read *Safe for drinking.* Perhaps one day we will again be able to see clearly to the bottom, twenty feet down. Hopefully, the Americans will adopt measures as stringent as the Canadian ones and clean their channel, too.

Whether the Canadian riverbank will long remain free of intensive commercial development is, however, another matter. A New York bank advertises, "You can be better than you are"—implying that having money makes all the difference, as indeed it seems to have done, because there is a difference between the two sides of the river. There is a commercial strip culture all along the American shore. Today there are cliffs and forests, marshes and quiet bays, deer, beavers, muskrats, and eagles on the Canadian side. Tomorrow there may be neon lights, condominiums, shopping centers, and Disneyland North. If a man who has worked hard all his life for the little he has should suddenly be offered $150,000 for his stony river-front acres, he might be tempted to accept. Then Mammon would enter the Garden.

Very shortly after that there would be no flight of ducks at dawn, no days spent at the very center of time. For two people moving slowly in a small boat among the islands there would be a view of billboards and the architecture of hamburger stands.

Such things have happened elsewhere.

The choice will be made here by the living, according to the strength of their bond to the dead.

16

The new boat needed a name, and we told the Creightons we were thinking of calling it the *Pecan*, because it was a tin boat the color of pea soup. We said this as we were moving more than a ton of coal from the Creightons' cellar. Since they had installed electric heating, they said the coal was ours if we would carry it away, and we shoveled it out of its bin into gunnysacks and cardboard cartons and loaded these into the boat. It was a process that required several trips, and it gave Bill an idea.

"Why don't you call it the *Coal Porter?*" he asked.

We thought it a marvelous pun till we told it to a young married couple. Their absolutely blank reaction was rather sobering. We then realized that no one could understand Bill's joke who lacked a personal memory of the 1930s and the songs and humor of the time. The young people not only lacked such a memory, but they also lacked any knowledge of a day when most city houses were fired by coal furnaces and when there were porters. We were, apparently, growing older.

The boat was still without a name when our son and his wife arrived to visit, and Chris took Wendy fishing. All her life a city girl, Wendy was new to the mysteries of rod and reel, boats and water. But once she was introduced to them, avenues opened before her. Their first hour on the water failed to produce a fish. It was Christopher's opinion, based on his experience, that the fish were not biting. He, for one, was going to stop and swim instead. Wendy said she would rather continue fishing, and could she take the boat out by herself? Since she was new to the river and boats and their dangers, we said yes, but to stay close by our island, drifting along its flanks, casting toward the rocks, and to call if she needed help.

None of us heard her shrieking. Margaret and I were in the kitchen; Chris was changing his clothes in a bedroom. We did, however, see Wendy return. She ran the outboard around in a circle, and we thought she did not know how to steer it. We went to the dock to help her land, but she did not need it; she had run around in circles to attract our attention, she said. She held up a broken rod. She was sorry she had broken it, she said, but all at once it had snapped; she had no idea why.

"Did you snag your line on bottom?" someone asked.

"No, it was a huge fish," Wendy said. "It kept pulling and pulling and then the rod broke."

"It was an old rod anyway," I told her. "Don't worry about the rod. How big do you think it was?"

"Oh, I didn't lose the fish," she said.

She scrambled forward, and from beneath the bow deck she pushed into view an enormous pike that flopped about on the metal hull. Chris jumped down into the boat to grasp the fish before it flopped overboard.

"He bounced around like that when I got him in," Wendy said. "I didn't know what else to do, so I sat on him and called for you, but no one heard me. I couldn't run the boat, sitting on the fish, so I got him up underneath there where he couldn't jump out."

Everyone told her she had done exactly the right thing, which seemed to make Wendy feel much better. Until then she had seemed apprehensive.

"What kind is it?" she asked. "Is it good to eat?"

How she managed to land that fish will be one of life's enduring mysteries. By all odds, when the rod broke there should have been no way of playing the fish till it tired, and just the dead weight of it should have broken the four-pound-test monofilament line—to say nothing of the force the fish would have exerted as it thrashed about in the water. Nor could anyone understand why the rod had broken; perhaps it was old. But there was the fish, with the lure still in its mouth, and a tangle of monofilament all over the boat, and Wendy all excited and pleased.

"Get a scaler and the knife out of the baitbox, and I'll show you how to clean it," Chris said.

We now had a name for the new aluminum out-board. We should have thought of it at once. There was the *Margaret,* named for the first two women to appear in the family, and the *Tory,* named for Victoria. Now there was the *Wendy,* in honor of the island's newest fisherwoman.

"I've never had a boat named after me before," Wendy said. She seemed quite favorably impressed.

It is always a pleasure to have the children on the island, although I suppose that Chris and Wendy and Margaret and Kirk are not our children in the sense that each has a separate adult identity, and that each couple has also that special, mutual identity that partners to a marriage take on. The same could be said of Victoria and her fiancé, Michael, who at this writing plan to be married on the island before an altar set beneath great white pines. Living on the island with us during their engagement, they too began to take on that special third person that is the bonded pair; we could see the process at work day by day—the formation of a mutual alliance and a united front to the world. But they are all our children in the sense of human inheritance. They all come to the island whenever they can, not so much to see us as to live an artless while in man's natural home where, during the past twenty years, they have seen a family home created.

We are particularly delighted to see new beginnings being made all over again, discoveries rediscovered, new rules and namings and rituals formed to celebrate the same mystery. It would only be in the natural order of things if small new swimmers should one day splash off toward Fancy Rock, remembering to make cups of their hands. So I would hope, without particular concern as to whether the small new swimmers belonged to our family, so long as some family lived on the island and there were children.

We have no children on the island in fall. They come in summer, bringing gifts for the house, to help with the painting, the wood chopping and the chores, to swim and fish, touch familiar bases. The house is full of color, sound, and movement while they are here and considerably more orderly after they have left. Then we are left alone to savor the long golden light and colors of fall until the winter comes.

17

The end of our island year usually comes when water freezes in the drains and in the kitchen sink. By that time the refrigerator will long since have been turned off; we will have been wearing heavy clothing for some weeks and sleeping under blankets and quilt. I will have moved my books and work into the living room, for there is no heat in the little cottage at the head of the island, and I cannot type while wearing gloves. We will be warm enough in the living room with fires in hearth and stove, but it will be cold enough to wear a parka down the hall to bed. There will be frost every night. The river will be very low, with skim ice forming in the shallow protected bays, and there will be days of northeast gales.

The lowering river is a nuisance and a danger. It is a nuisance to us because we are both somewhat less athletic than we were twenty years ago. We can no longer reach up to grasp the edging of a dock that is higher than our heads and haul ourselves out of a boat by a process akin to chinning. Now we nail blocks of wood to our dock stavings to serve as footholds and grasp a rope, rigged from an overhead beam in the boathouse, to steady our balance. With wry derision we call it the Granny Rope. Steps and rope minimize the danger of our falling several feet into a boat while climbing in or out of it, but the more important danger that the lowering river represents is that of running on rocks and shoals. This is particularly true at night, when distances are deceptive. You may think you have allowed sufficient room for the shoal you know to be there, but the shoal is more extensively exposed and larger in area than in times of summer water depth. If in addition to the inconvenience, difficulty and danger of low water, the weather should turn nasty although not freezing and remain foul for a fortnight, then we may call an end to our island year without waiting for the ice to come. One year it all ended not with a whimper but a bang.

There was never a more wretched Saturday afternoon: blue-black skies, a rising northeast gale, the trees bare, intermittent rain spattering against the house, and every promise of worse to come. Margaret and I went out on the now screenless front porch to read the barometer and stand for a moment in the gale.

The only boat on the water, and possibly the only cruiser in the area not in winter drydock, a large craft as out of season as a skier in August, was running flat out in heavy seas, sending up shell bursts of spray as it sped on the wrong side of a red buoy that marks a shoal a thousand yards east of our island. Possibly the skipper could not see the red stick in the smother. Perhaps in the dark day it looked like a black stick to him. He was in any case running too close to whatever kind of buoy it might have been.

"He's going to hit the shoal!"

"He's going to hit it!"

The cruiser lifted. It rose out of the water and fell back before we heard the dull whump of it striking rock.

"Let's go," I told Margaret.

"Let me turn the lamps out," she said.

We never leave an oil lamp burning when no one is on the island.

"They may be hurt," I said.

"I'll put the lamps out," she said.

I did not wait for her but ran down the hall and stairs, into the boathouse, cast loose the *Margaret*'s lines, swung down into the boat, started the engine, cursed all women, lamps, cruisers, and their skippers, and backed out of the boat slip and into the gale.

No one else was going to get him. There were no other boats on the water, and this late in the year there were no other eyes on the river than ours.

The cruiser was rolling heavily in the troughs. It had gone completely across the shoal and was now drifting down the wind. I approached cautiously; the cruiser was some thirty feet long and it would drift faster than the smaller, lower *Margaret*. When it came time to throw a line, I did not want the hulk bearing down on me.

The skipper came out of the cabin to stand on the bow.

I could see him shout to me.

I came as close as I dared, shut off the engine, and called. Yes, he did want a tow. He had lost both power and steering. Fortunately, no one was hurt. He did not think he was sinking.

All this was conveyed in shoutings as our boats rolled in the gale. I threw him the *Margaret*'s long, heavy towing line, and when he had cleated it to his bow, I felt the weight of a six-ton cruiser in a northeast blow. If I were to tow him across river, either to Alexandria Bay or to Rockport, I would have to crab across miles of water in a worsening storm. The simplest thing would be to take him to our island. The only trick would be to gauge the weight of the cruiser and the force of waves and wind so as to leave him dead in the water precisely beside our swimming dock.

I could not get it right on the first pass, and Margaret, standing on the boathouse dock in the rain, was horrified to see the towed cruiser swing toward our rocky shore.

The cruiser just barely cleared a jumble of stone.

But on the next pass, there he was, dead in the water as fine as you please, an inch or two off that eight-foot-long bit of dock.

The cruiser's skipper leaped down and cleated his vessel to its mooring smartly enough, but in the dark and the wind the *Margaret* drifted down over the tow rope, fouling the propeller.

Now I was the mariner in distress, and Margaret had to come out in the *Tory* to rescue me. We shouted to each other in the rainy dark; there were misunderstandings and bleak words and a great deal of difficulty getting the boats into their slips. We were wet, cold, and tired of the job when all was done at last. I somewhat unfairly thought none of the last bit would have happened if Margaret had come out with me instead of fiddling with those lamps. Margaret's view was that I should have waited for her.

The cruiser rode easily at its mooring, the cabin lights aglow. The skipper, his wife and two children were still a bit frightened. They said it was lucky we had seen them, and we agreed. If sheer chance had not led us out on the porch at a particular moment, we never would have seen them. Nor would anyone else. They would have drifted helpless in the gale until their cruiser banged upon the stones of someone's deserted island— and then their real problems would have begun. They seemed safe enough now; they had lost their twin propellers and twin rudders to the shoal and perhaps had put a hole in their outer hull, but no water was coming through the inner hull, and they could stay at our swimming dock for the night.

The next morning I took the skipper to Alexandria Bay to arrange for the cruiser to be towed there by the people who would repair her. When I returned to the island, Margaret told me we were leaving.

The whole episode had been disturbing to her. She

felt we were very lucky to have done something we were not equipped to do. We were not in the rescue business. The people who were had special equipment, heavier, more powerful boats, knowledge, and experience. She should not have been asked to fend heaving boats off docks. Some years earlier she had an operation for a slipped disc, and she did not want to go back to the hospital. I should have known better. The whole thing had been too exciting. Furthermore, she said, the river was low, it was difficult to get in and out of boats now, the weather was vile, it was growing colder, and since none of this would get any better, we were now leaving.

I thought the rescue had been simple and straight-forward enough. I could see her point about not asking her to break her back, and it was certainly true that the weather was deteriorating. But I always dislike having to leave the island.

The last of our rituals is sad. It goes quickly enough, and there's another pity, because it does not seem right to be able so quickly to take apart what has taken so long to put together. The curtains come down from the windows, the pictures from the walls. The porch furniture is brought into the living room; old, torn pillowcases and sheets are white shrouds draped over the Aladdin lamps and furniture. Dishes, cups, saucers, and glasses are turned upside down on their shelves; the door of the empty refrigerator is propped ajar; poison is set out in the kitchen and in each of the other rooms against the intrusion of rodents. Boat cushions from the *Margaret* are stored in a bedroom, fishing tackle in closets. The screens come down, the shutters go up. The typewriter, books, paper, and the packed bags are carried down to the cushionless *Margaret* and stowed aboard. There is a last check through the now lifeless, shrouded rooms, locking the kitchen door from the inside, closing all the doors one after another down the hall, locking the front door. In the boathouse there is the hot-water heater to turn off and the supply of bottle gas. The water lines are drained. The door to the boat slips is locked.

We take the *Margaret* across the river to the Huck marina and leave her there. The Hucks will take her back, haul her out with a chainfalls, storing her and the *Tory* and the *Wendy* on timbers placed across the empty boat slips, and close the boathouse doors and drop their bars in place. In the winter that comes to the island, the snow may drift to the second-story windows. Visitors will come across the ice: varying hare, ermine, foxes, the coyotes the river people call timber wolves, and red and black squirrels. The voles and meadow mice will be snugly quartered beneath the snow. Deer will come tiptoeing across the frozen river and pause among our trees.

We never look back when we leave the island.

Envoi

One evening in fall a city friend and I stood on the overhanging porch of my island house, fascinated by the curious light. The moon, rising round and full, was escaping the silhouettes of the black oaks while, at the same time, a huge red sun was settling into the arms of the pines on the Canadian mainland. Behind the moon the sky was a deep purple. In the west, it was still broad light. In between, there was a gray-scarlet haze.

As we watched, a lone fishing boat came across the still water—water so quiet that it reflected the moon, the clouds, the islands, and the sun. As the boat crossed the river downstream from the island, there rose from the water shapes we had not seen before, so perfectly had their colors blended into the reflections and into that strange dusk.

But up they came, breaking into the air, more than fifty of them, quickly and silently gaining altitude until, just over our house, they gave those cries that have been called honks but which more often sound like hound puppies yelping, and in obedience to these commands the geese aligned themselves into their skein, a V with one short and one immensely long leg, and wheeled overhead, bound southwest into the setting sun.

We watched till we could see them no more. My friend seemed perplexed.

"Tell me," he said at last. "Is this the real world, or is the city the real world?"

Of course the answer is that both worlds are equally real. They are, however, different. They are so different that the question comes again and again, not only to the minds of our friends but also to our own.

I do not know where the geese go when they leave the river in fall, or what they do when they are wherever they are in winter, or which of their residences seems more real, or more like home to them, or if they have a home at all, or if they feel generally at home in all the world. I can, however, say something of ourselves.

Wherever we are in winter, and however necessary it is for us to be there, we look forward to spring. Then, as soon as we return to the river, we feel as if we had never been away.

As soon as we are on the water, moving toward our island, we somehow re-enter an endless moment in time. The islands have not moved, the river moves past them as it has always done, the wind leans across the water and tangles in the trees. Shoals of panfish sway in the gray-green light in the boat slips; birds hunt through the air and among the birches. They are still burning the missionary on the golf course and the raft with the oak is breaking up in the storm. George Boldt is building his castle and the schoolteacher is still rowing her skiffload of whisky across the river at night to relieve the thirst of America during Prohibition. We are young and our children are going to school in their little scarlet boat; it is our daughter's wedding day, and there are Will and Effie, setting off downriver on the ice in their sleigh. All that has happened is still happening, together with all that is happening at the moment. Nothing has changed in this always new and infinitely old center of our lives. We never feel homeless in winter because we know where we live. We live in a house on a stone in the middle of a river in the center of the world at the very heart of time.

ABOUT THE AUTHOR

John Keats is one of the nation's best-known social critics. His acerbic books on major domestic issues such as the tyranny of the automobile (*The Insolent Chariots*), the dark side of suburbia (*The Crack in the Picture Window*), and our excessive zeal for college education regardless of the student's aptitude (*The Sheepskin Psychosis*) have yielded valuable corrective insights and added pointed new phrases to the language.

Mr. Keats left newspaper work in 1953 to become a free-lance writer. In *Of Time and an Island* he reflects on these last twenty years and on the perspective life on an island has given him on life in the larger world. When he is not at home on Pine Island, he lives variously on an island in Italy, or in the British Isles, or in Philadelphia. Among his other books are a biography of Dorothy Parker (*You Might as Well Live*) and a history of the Louisiana Purchase (*Eminent Domain*). He is married and has three children.

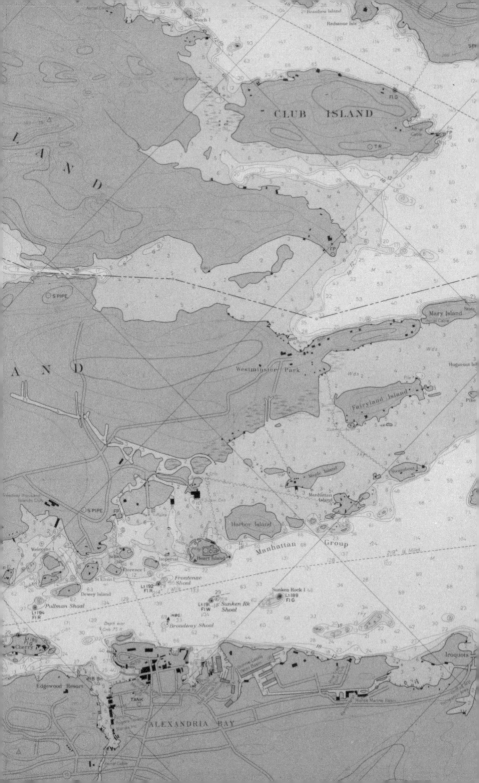